HIKING TRAILS III

Northern Vancouver Island

Great Central Lake to Cape Scott

featuring
Strathcona Park
and for the first time
Malcolm Island
Nootka Island
and
the **Beaufort Range**

NINTH EDITION, 2002

Published by the Vancouver Island
Trails Information Society
(VITIS)

Revised and expanded by
Richard K. Blier

Ninth edition copyright © 2002 Vancouver Island Trails Information Society
Revised and expanded by Richard K. Blier
Original copyright © 1975
Outdoor Club of Victoria Trails Information Society
Compiled and edited by Jane Waddell
Revised and reprinted 1975, 1977, 1979, 1982, 1986
Reprinted with revision notes 1990
Revised and expanded 1992, by James Rutter
Reprinted 1994
Vancouver Island Trails Information Society (society name change only)
Revised and expanded 1996, by James Rutter
Revised and expanded 2002, by Richard K. Blier

Map revision: A.N. Fraser Drafting Services, Victoria, BC
Illustrations: John S.T. Gibson, Judy Trousdell and Susan Lawrence
Photos: Richard K. Blier
Editing and layout: Susan Lawrence
Map digitization, book design and formatting: Desktop Publishing Ltd., Victoria, BC
Printed and bound in Canada by Friesens, Altona, Manitoba
Distribution: Orca Book Publishers, Victoria, BC

Vancouver Island Trails Information Society (VITIS)
web page: www.hikingtrailsbooks.com
e-mail: vanisletrails@uniserve.com
telephone: Victoria area 598-0003
toll free 1-866-598-0003
fax: Victoria area 474-4577
toll free 1-866-474-4577

National Library of Canada Cataloguing in Publication Data

Main entry under title:
Hiking trails III
Includes bibliographical references and index.
ISBN 0-9697667-4-2
1. Trails—British Columbia—Vancouver Island—Guidebooks. 2.
Hiking—British Columbia—Vancouver Island—Guidebooks. 3. Vancouver
Island (B.C.)—Guidebooks. I. Blier, Richard K., 1952- II. Vancouver Island
Trails Information Society.
GV 199.44.C22V35 2002 917.11'2044 C2002-910994-9

List of Maps

Strathcona Provincial Park Maps:

Base maps (printed in grey and blue) for the Strathcona Provincial Park topographical maps have been reproduced using overlays from National Topographical Series (NTS) © produced under license from Her Majesty the Queen in Right of Canada, with permission of Natural Resources Canada.
The overlay information printed in black has been drawn by Arnold Fraser of A.N. Fraser Drafting Services, who prepared all the other maps.

COVER PHOTOGRAPH: Hikers on Forbidden Plateau in Strathcona Park, with Mount Albert Edward in the background.
Photo courtesy of Ron Quilter of BC Parks.

Strathcona Park was named after Donald Alexander Smith, instrumental in the building of the CPR; Member of Parliament, 1971; knighted in 1866; Governor of the HBC, 1889; appointed Canada's high commissioner in England, 1896; made Lord Strathcona and Mount Royal, 1897. Strathcona Park is the oldest of BC's provincial parks, and it contains Vancouver Island's highest peak and Canada's highest waterfall. **Mount Albert Edward** was named after Queen Victoria's eldest son, who ascended the throne as Edward VII after her death in 1901.

Maps of other areas:

Contents

Contents

Contents

Legend

Throughout these maps we have used the following legend:

——————— Public road or highway

—— — —— Gravel or dirt road

— — — — — Clearly defined trail

•••••••••••• Hiking route requiring map and compass
(experienced hikers only)

⚑ Provincial Park campground

⛺ Campsite with pit toilet (s)

△ backcountry campsite (no facilities)

⊙ Memorial cairn

■ Cabin

(T) Toilet only

(W) Water source (treat before use)

⚒ Mine

P Parking

(V) Viewpoint

▽ Fee Collection Station

Note: Contour lines on our maps are at different intervals:
500-foot intervals: Map A0 Gold Lake
                            Map 10 Schoen Lake Provincial Park
100-metre intervals: Map 2A Mount Joan / Mount Curran
40-metre intervals: all other topographical maps

Conversions: 500 ft = 152.4 m   100 m = 328 ft   40 m = 131.2 ft

Note: Wherever the text references a specific location with a superscript (raised number) like this: Tatsno Lakes[47], a corresponding circled number will be found on a map in this book.

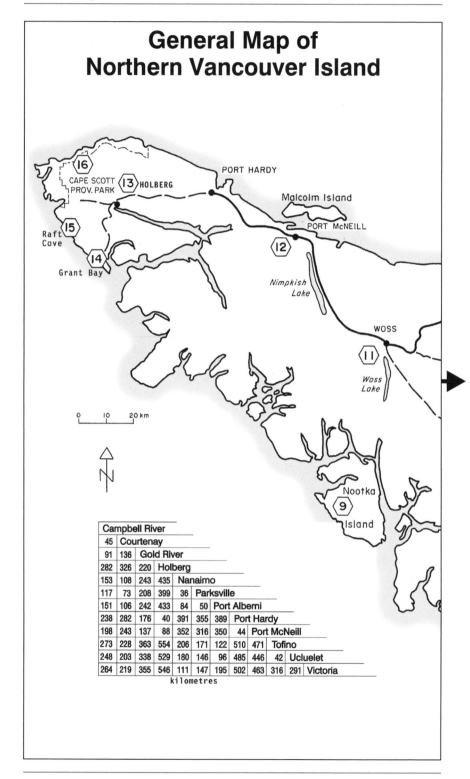

General Map of Northern Vancouver Island

Campbell River											
45	Courtenay										
91	136	Gold River									
282	326	220	Holberg								
153	108	243	435	Nanaimo							
117	73	208	399	36	Parksville						
151	106	242	433	84	50	Port Alberni					
238	282	176	40	391	355	389	Port Hardy				
198	243	137	88	352	316	350	44	Port McNeill			
273	228	363	554	206	171	122	510	471	Tofino		
248	203	338	529	180	146	96	485	446	42	Ucluelet	
264	219	355	546	111	147	195	502	463	316	291	Victoria

kilometres

Key to Maps of Trails and Routes

Maps A0-E5	Strathcona Provincial Park
Map 1	Clayoquot Sound and Western Strathcona Provincial Park
Maps 2A, 2B	Beaufort Range
Map 3	Seal Bay Regional Nature Park
Maps 4A, 4B	Quadra Island
Map 5	Campbell River Area
Map 6	Snowden Demonstration Forest
Map 7	Sayward Forest
Map 8b	Upana Caves
Maps 9A, 9B	Nootka Trail

Map 10 Schoen Lake Provincial Park
Map 11 Nimpkish Valley
Map 12 Port McNeill/Malcolm Island
Map 13 Port Hardy/Holberg Area
Map 14 Grant Bay
Map 15 Raft Cove Provincial Park
Maps 16A, 16B Cape Scott Provincial Park

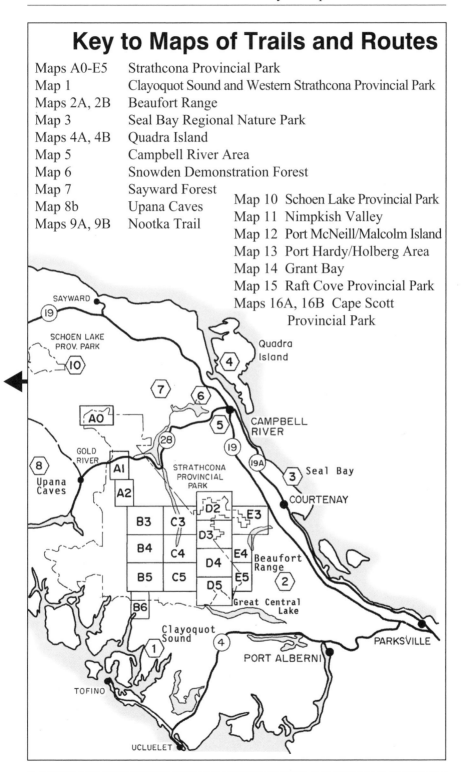

Editor's Note

Although *Hiking Trails III* covers all of Vancouver Island north of Parksville, Qualicum, and Port Alberni, for years the heart of the book has been the trails and routes of Strathcona Provincial Park, which itself covers over 250,000 ha. Our thanks go out once again to the principal contributors to the original version of this book: **John S.T. Gibson, John W.E. Harris, Dan Hicks, Ruth Masters, Jack Shark** and **Syd Watts**; to the two previous editors, **Jane Waddell** and **James Rutter**; and to the many others who contributed to the original compilation in 1975 and to subsequent revisions.

Throughout the years and the book's various editions, dedicated hikers and climbers have contributed accurate descriptions of trail conditions, offered detailed trip accounts, suggested corrections, and pointed the way to new hiking destinations. The 9th Edition of *Hiking Trails III* is no exception. Many people went out of their way to ensure that my map and text queries were answered correctly, and that I met my deadlines. Their efforts made my job a lot easier. Special thanks go to the following who have provided key updates for this edition: **Brian Allaert, Chris Barner, Sandy Briggs, Carl Butterworth, Lindsay Elms, Dorthea Hangaard, Pal Horvath, Annemarie Koch, Kent Krauza, Noel Lax, Glenn G. Lewis, Ruth Masters, Graeme McFadyen, Jeff Mosher, Lynda Nagle, Ron Quilter, S. J. Rhodes, Ken Rodonets, Peter Rothermel, Keith Seguin, Clayton Smith, Steve Smith, Philip Stone, Jim Spowart, Jim Thompson, Thom Ward, Syd Watts, Nicki Westarp** and members of various **Vancouver Island hiking and mountaineering clubs**.

For valuable assistance and information I thank: **BC Forest Service, BC Parks, Canadian Forest Products, Federation of Mountain Clubs of BC, Land Data BC, Ministry of Water, Lands and Air Protection, Ministry of Sustainable Resource Management, Outdoor Recreation Council of BC, local regional districts and tourist infocentres, TimberWest, Western Forest Products** and **Weyerhaeuser** (formerly MacMillan Bloedel).

Thanks go to **Arnold Fraser** who once again deciphered my scribbles, circles and arrows on the map updates to create the maps and overlays for this edition. Finally, as always, I have special thanks for the VITIS Editorial Committee members, **George Broome, Joyce Folbigg, John W.E. Harris, Aldyth Hunter, Susan Lawrence** and **Ron Weir**, and to the other Society members, **Betty Burroughs** and **Irm Houle**.

Readers who have information that would be useful to other hikers are encouraged to send in updates on trails and routes for inclusion in subsequent revisions. Please relay any information to vanisletrails@uniserve.com.

After compiling this 9th Edition I feel I know northern Vancouver Island's hiking destinations a little bit better. I hope *Hiking Trails III* leaves you with that impression too.

Richard K. Blier (July, 2002)

See *About the Editor*, page 224.

About The Vancouver Island Trails Information Society (VITIS)

The Vancouver Island Trails Information Society is a non-profit society dedicated to providing accurate information to the public about trails and parks on Vancouver Island.

The society has its origins in the Outdoor Club of Victoria. OCV members, especially Dr. Jim Fiddess and Ted Fairhurst, had long dreamed of producing a book about the trails known and used by their club. Their dreams came true in 1971 with the formation of a hard-working committee. The new editor was to be Jane Waddell, ably assisted by Bill Burroughs, John Harris, Dave Birch and Jane Toms, among others.

The group incorporated as a non-profit society, the Outdoor Club of Victoria Trails Information Society, and produced its first book, HIKING TRAILS, Victoria and Southern Vancouver Island, in December of 1972. It proved to be an outstanding success, and by 1975 books on central and northern Vancouver Island had followed. Updated editions of each of these books are available. *Hiking Trails I: Victoria and Vicinity* covers the Capital Regional District, and *Hiking Trails II: South-Central Vancouver Island and the Gulf Islands* covers the Gulf Islands and the south-central portion of Vancouver Island from Koksilah River Park to Mount Arrowsmith and west to Pacific Rim National Park Reserve.

In 1993, in an effort to better describe the scope of its work, and to eliminate confusion, the society changed its name to the Vancouver Island Trails Information Society (VITIS).

For more information about VITIS:
e-mail: vanisletrails@uniserve.com;
or visit: www.hikingtrailsbooks.com.

telephone: Victoria area 598-0003   toll free 1-866-598-0003
fax: Victoria area 474-4577   toll free 1-866-474-4577

How To Use This Book

Hiking Trails III describes trails and wilderness routes in some of the most beautiful areas of northern and central Vancouver Island. We make no attempt here to recommend the sort of equipment, clothing or food that a backpacking trip entails, as there are many books and guides available that do this, and other enthusiasts to offer you conflicting opinions. Preparing for a trip can be as much fun as the trip itself and we hope we are supplying here something to help you properly do your homework on route and trail conditions **before** setting out.

This guide will help you to discover the joys of hiking, but it is a hiker's guide only and it will not show you how to climb the highest peaks. You have to do that for yourself. Instead we emphasize a need for self-reliance. Self-reliant hikers will have an experienced leader, and also the right maps, a good compass and the know-how to use them both. They will also carry a first aid kit, some overnight survival gear and be able to deal with any emergency.

Hiking Trails III provides a key to the door, a portal beyond which you are on your own. It is essential that you read the text rather than simply try to follow the dots on our maps. Though brief, the wilderness route descriptions are perhaps the most valuable part of this book. Every word was written by someone who was there, and who experienced the same difficulties now facing you. Many have pinpointed GPS co-ordinates, confirmed in the field, for use on our maps. As you enjoy these trails and routes, may you hike safely and step lightly.

Our text should be read in conjunction with our maps, and also the corresponding National Topographical Series (NTS) 1:50,000 maps. References to altitude and compass directions are frequently used to pinpoint position. **Wherever the text references a specific location with a superscript (raised number) like this: Tatsno Lakes[47], a corresponding circled number will be found on a map in this book.** Numbers converted to metric have been rounded off. Times given are average group times as taken over the years by experienced parties, carrying packs.

For the benefit of newcomers to hiking, a trail is a way that may have been built by man or travelled regularly by animals so it is obvious. Trails are sometimes signed, marked with cairns or flagged with tape. Routes indicate a possible way to go, though on the ground there may be nothing to see, except the lie of the land as understood by an experienced hiker. Our maps show trails and routes, and only experienced hikers or groups with very experienced leaders should attempt to follow the wilderness routes.

We will not be held responsible for any discrepancies, inaccuracies or omissions, as conditions and road access are constantly changing. Hikers always travel at their own risk and it is up to the individual to check current conditions.

Vancouver Island Trails Information Society (VITIS)

Hints and Cautions

Most of British Columbia's provincial forests are owned by the public and leased and managed by forest companies. Recreation (camping and picnicking) sites and trails, developed by the BC Forest Service (BCFS) and logging companies on provincial forestlands, are managed for multiple use. Within provincial parks, BC Parks has developed campsites in order to focus the impact of an ever-increasing number of visitors, many from other countries around the world. **Throughout this book we use the term "frontcountry" to denote regions with serviced campsites, usually close to the main roads. "Backcountry" refers to more remote areas, with wilderness campsites and no amenities.** Those venturing into northern Vancouver Island's backcountry areas for the first time will appreciate the following selection of hints and cautions. Even experienced hikers will benefit from some of our quick reminders.

Access information on logging roads may be obtained from company division offices, tourism offices or from BCFS offices. (See pages 21-24.) Ask locally for recreation and logging road guides. Due to problems with narrow roads, vandalism or fire hazard, access to logging roads is often limited. Roads may be "**open**", with travel permitted at all times; "**restricted**" (limited), with travel permitted only during non-working hours (normally from about 5:00 pm to 6:30 am, and on week-ends and holidays); or "closed". Access restrictions may change frequently with little notice. Loggers sometimes work holidays and weekends. Roads are generally closed when fire hazard is high, or are open only in the mornings, even when general BCFS closures are not in effect. A long distance call a day or two in advance of a trip is often a worthwhile investment. Obey posted signs. Some open gates may be locked later when you need to leave.

Always have your vehicle's headlights on when travelling **logging roads**. These dirt and gravel arteries can be extremely dusty. If you're sharing the road with industrial traffic and a logging truck is approaching, the safest procedure is to pull well over to the side of the road and wait until the oncoming traffic has passed. Trucks often travel in groups so don't be in a hurry to pull back onto the road after one has passed. Always yield to loaded trucks, particularly on narrow roads and when they are travelling downhill. This may mean backing rapidly to a turn-off.

Exercise special care in remote areas. Many regions in this book are out of reach of immediate help in emergencies. Cell phones are unreliable in mountainous regions, valleys or away from population centres. Most logging vehicles carry radios and there are telephones at logging camps, but the major parks do not have offices and the trails are generally not patrolled regularly by park staff. Gasoline is not available away from main public roads and towns.

Maps: A contour line is simply all the points of the same elevation joined together, so when contour lines are close together it indicates that the terrain is steeper than where the lines are farther apart. This is most useful for determining where you are, as you can readily assess steepness, locate creeks and ridges, and calculate the effort that will be required. A contour (topographical) map and aerial photograph are useful adjuncts to the *trail* descriptions in this book; for the hiking *route* section they are essential.

National Topographical Series (NTS) maps at a scale of 1:50,000 (2 cm = 1 km) have been used for the base maps in this book. You should purchase your own because we have not reproduced all their information. (For example, NTS maps show forests in green, and the tree line is a good navigational map feature. TRIM maps 1:20,000 are also reliable references. (See *Map Sources* starting on page 21.)

Note: While all distances and elevations given in our text are in metric, **two topographical maps (Map A0 Gold Lake and Map 10 Schoen Lake Provincial Park) still show elevations in feet** on the grey (base) layer.

A compass is also useful, since even on a trail you can easily lose your way, especially in fog. At the least, a compass can keep you from going in circles. Remember, though trails are generally well marked, they tend to become hard to follow or even obliterated in places by slides, periodic flooding or tree blowdowns. Many hikers now use a **GPS**. These devices should be used with a map and compass, not as a replacement.

When **traversing active glaciers** always carry and use adequate lengths of rope. Watch for hidden crevasses, particularly in the spring or after a snowfall when a thin snow cover may camouflage these hazards.

The wise hiker travels with a friend in case of accident and leaves a trip plan, including time of return, with someone reliable. Extra food, even on day hikes, may come in handy. You should stay on trails unless absolutely sure where you are going. Be aware of the danger of being mistaken for a wild animal during hunting season, though hunting is not permitted within any of Vancouver Island's provincial parks. Good clothing, particularly strong footwear, is fundamental; waterproof matches, fire starter, maps, compass, a basic first aid kit, mosquito repellent and rainwear are essentials.

Don't expect trails to be well marked. As you go, glance back occasionally. Because the terrain often looks quite different when facing the other way, that will help you recognize features as you return. Plants grow slowly in alpine areas, and places trampled by careless feet recover only gradually. Stay on paths where these exist. Never roll rocks over cliffs as there might be someone below.

Do not build any campfires. Campfire-related activities such as off-trail wood collection, burn scars and incompletely burned garbage make campfires the single most-damaging human impact on sensitive areas. Always practice low-impact camping and use stoves in order to help protect the natural environment. **Once the Park Master Plan update is signed off (pending, 2002) new regulations will prohibit campfires anywhere in the backcountry of Strathcona Provincial Park, including the Elk River Valley. Currently, no fires are allowed in the Bedwell Lake / Price Creek corridor and Forbidden Plateau's core area. Fires will be permitted only at designated fire rings at high-use campgrounds (such as the Buttle Lake and Ralph River campsites on Buttle Lake) and various marine sites.**

Water from lakes, streams and rivers may be of dubious quality. Always boil, treat or filter your drinking water.

Thieves. Do not leave valuables in your car. Vehicles parked at a trailhead seem to be a target for thieves, who operate even during daytime. Many great hiking trips have been ruined as a consequence.

There is no one to pick up garbage so you must pack out all your paper, cans, etc. If you can, also take with you any other garbage left by thoughtless campers, especially bottles and cans. You will be helping greatly. Some areas are natural camping spots, and attract many people; if common sense and low impact camping techniques are not used these sites can be ruined for those who come later.

There are no **sanitary or toilet facilities** provided in most remote areas away from roads so come prepared. A small, collapsible shovel is useful. An ice axe can also be a multi-use tool! Ruth Masters, who was an architect of the first edition of this book, and has contributed to all subsequent editions, offers her own suggestions – see overleaf.

John W.E. Harris

Ruthie's Wilderness Cozy Can

"Haven't you all toiled your way to an exquisite camping spot, only to find toilet paper behind every bush? People who would not consider having non-matching fixtures or clashing tile colours in their home bathrooms, often behave like barbarians in the bush, and they also fail to train their kids in decent outdoor behaviour.

Upon arrival in camp it usually takes me less than half an hour to set up my exclusively designed outdoor biffy. Selecting a secluded spot reasonably close to camp, I tie a pole securely between two trees, at an acceptable height for the toilet seat, and I scratch out the hole with my walking stick/ice axe. Then I gather a plastic bag of sand or forest floor "duff" for "buryings". Lastly, I hang orange flagging tape at the entry trail for the "stop" and "go" signal. Remember, if the flag is up, you are in; if it's down, you're out.

On breaking camp it takes only a few seconds to dismantle my loo and tidy over the site. I take enormous pride in my wilderness biffies, which are definitely not to be sniffed at."

Ruth Masters

Editor's Note: A good guidebook on outdoor sanitation practices and procedures is Kathleen Meyer's ***How To Shit In The Woods*** published by Ten Speed Press.

Ruth takes a holiday at her own convenience.

Creatures Great and Small

Those who venture beyond their own back yards within the urban landscape trespass into the back yards of a myriad of native wildlife, animals ranging in size from tiny to intimidating.

There are no wild poisonous snakes on Vancouver Island, but mosquitoes and flies can be a serious nuisance. Many hikers choose to use an insect repellent. Wasps should be avoided; they nest in the ground and in bag-like nests in trees. Many people are allergic to the stings of insects and plants, so pack any necessary antidotes. In a moderate climate, ticks may be encountered at almost any time of the year, but they are most numerous when the weather warms in late spring. Ticks are arachnids, related to spiders, mites and scorpions. Most ticks have life cycles that include stages of: egg, six-legged larva, eight-legged nymph and eight-legged adult, with each stage taking from days to years, depending on conditions. All ticks are parasitic, but they require different hosts for different stages, with large vertebrates (including humans) being on the menu of the adult female, who will latch on and drink blood until she is fully engorged. After mating, she drops to the ground, lays up to 10,000 eggs, and then dies. Local ticks do not carry Rocky Mountain spotted fever or tick paralysis, but western black-legged ticks, found on Vancouver Island, may carry the bacteria responsible for Lyme disease. Between 1991 and 2001, 59 cases of Lyme disease were reported in BC. A common early symptom of infection is a circular "bull's-eye" rash at the site of the bite. The disease can be cured by antibiotics, but if left untreated it can affect the joints, heart and nervous system. To prevent tick bites, hikers can cover up with long-sleeved shirts and full-length pants secured at the ankle; they can apply insect repellent containing Deet; and they can avoid brushy areas, keeping to open trails.

Although our resident black bears are rarely encountered (we have 13,000 black bears on the Island, but no grizzly bears), always use discretion in the woods of Vancouver Island, particularly in areas where food, such as berries, is available. Remember they are not the intruders, we are, and bears defend their personal space, their food, and their cubs. Even so, bears will generally do their best to avoid you if they hear you coming, so talking loudly and making other noises when hiking in suspicious areas is advised. Bears have an excellent sense of smell and of hearing, and, contrary to popular belief, very good eyesight. It is likely the bear sees you but you remain unaware of his presence. If you do see or hear bears, give them a wide berth and leave the area immediately; if you are actually approached, act large and make lots of noise. Move slowly away and avoid eye contact. A bear can run as fast as a horse, uphill or down, and black bears are good tree-climbers. When camping, store food away from camp, never in your tent. Don't sleep in the clothes you wore to cook food. It is best not to take children or dogs into bear country. Because BC is home to about 160,000 black bears, the Wildlife Branch of the former BC Ministry of Environment, Lands and Parks produced two pamphlets: *Safety Guide to Bears in the Wild* and *Safety Guide to Bears at Your Home*, both of which may still be available. This is black bear country.

Vancouver Island is also cougar country, though you can live your whole life here and never see one. Sightings are rare and confrontations are extremely rare. Even so, in the last century there have been more than two dozen attacks on humans by cougars on Vancouver Island, with three fatalities. Generally, these attacks have been on children, with the attack on an adult cyclist near Port Alice being a recent exception. Cougars are big animals, with males weighing 60-90 kg and females, 40-50 kg. They are fast and strong and they are predators. Their prey is primarily deer, but includes other animals, large and small. Children are probably the most common human target because their size, sounds and movements resemble those of other prey animals. Cougars are most active at dawn and dusk, but will roam and hunt during any time of the day or night. They may be encountered at any time of the year, but the likelihood of contact increases in late spring and summer when yearlings leave their mother to establish their own territory. Avoidance is the best defence. Hike in groups and make your presence known. Keep children in the centre of your group, never running ahead or trailing behind. If you come across cougar prints, scat, or a buried food cache, leave the area immediately. If you actually encounter a cougar, do not run. Stay put and stay calm. Allow the cougar an escape route. Gather up and protect children. Face the animal, maintain eye contact, and make yourself look and sound large. Stand tall, wave branches; do not crouch or turn your back. If the cougar acts aggressive, stand your ground and make yourself look and sound strong, more like a threat than a meal. If you are attacked, fight back with any means at your disposal. A cougar sighting is a rare and treasured event, one to be reported to friends and family; a cougar confrontation is a serious event, one to be reported to a Conservation Officer. The former Ministry of Environment, Lands and Parks produced a pamphlet, *Safety Guide to Cougars*; copies may still be available.

Vancouver Island supports a small population of gray, or timber, wolves. Although they have a highly developed social order within their packs, they tend to keep to themselves, posing no serious risk to humans. Unless you are foolish enough to leave food about where they can get at it, you are likely only to be aware of their presence by seeing their footprints, or hearing their eerie howls at night.

Susan Lawrence

Club Addresses

For information on the following Vancouver Island clubs:

- Alberni Valley Outdoor Club (AVOC)

- Alpine Club of Canada (ACC), Vancouver Island Section

- Comox District Mountaineering Club (CDMC)

- Heathens Mountaineering Club (HMC) (Campbell River)

- Island Mountain Ramblers (IMR) (Nanaimo)

- Outdoor Club of Victoria (OCV)

Contact: **The Federation of Mountain Clubs of BC** (FMCBC)
47 West Broadway, Vancouver, BC V5Y 1P1
(604) 878-7007; 1-888-892-2266 (toll-free)
e-mail: fmcbc@mountainclubs.bc
website: www.mountainclubs.bc.ca

or

The Outdoor Recreation Council of BC
334 - 1367 West Broadway, Vancouver, BC V6H 4A9
(604) 737-3058; fax (604) 737-3666
e-mail: orc@intergate.ca
website: www.orcbc.ca

Map Sources

Some logging company recreation maps are available. Check with local offices (see *Logging Companies* on page 24) and tourist infocentres. The **North Island Discovery Centre**, on Highway 19 near the Beaver Cove turnoff, is a good source of regional logging company maps. You can also register for free seasonal logging tours. For information contact: North Island Discovery Centre, Box 130, Port McNeill, BC V0N 2R0 (250) 956-3844; (250) 956-3848 (fax); e-mail: nifctour.island.net or visit www.island.net/~nifctour. The centre is open seasonally from late June to August 31st.

Some Search and Rescue organizations publish area recreation and logging road guides including: *Maps of the Comox Valley*, published by the Comox Valley Ground Search and Rescue Association, PO Box 3511, Courtenay, BC V9N 6Z8 (co-sponsored by the Comox Valley Chamber of Commerce); *Logging and Highway Road Map*, published by the Campbell River Search and Rescue Society, PO Box 705, Campbell River, BC V9W 6J3. Inquire locally at tourist infocentres.

Mussio Ventures' *Backroad Mapbook Volume II: Vancouver Island and the Gulf Islands* has detailed maps of the logging roads and covers outdoor recreation destinations on Vancouver Island.

For National Topographical Series (NTS) (1:50,000 scale) maps:

- Crown Publications, 521 Fort St., Victoria, BC V8W 1E7 (250) 386-4636

- Geological Survey Canada, 101 – 605 Robson St., Vancouver, BC V6B 5J3 (604) 666-0271

- International Travel Maps and Books, 530 West Broadway, Vancouver, BC V5Z 1E9 (604) 879-3621

- Island Blue Print, 905 Fort St., Victoria, BC V8V 3K3 (250) 385-9786; 1-800-661-3332 (toll-free)

- Mountain Meadows Sporting Goods, 368 Fifth St., Courtenay, BC V9N 1K1 (250) 338-8732; 1-866-882-8885 (toll-free)

- Nanaimo Maps and Charts*, 8 Church St., Nanaimo, BC V9R 5H4 1-800-665-2513 (toll-free)

- Robinson's Sporting Goods, 1307 Broad St., Victoria, BC V8W 2A8 (250) 385-3429

- Spinners Stores, Discovery Harbour Mall, 164 – 1436 Island Highway, Campbell River, BC V9W 8C9 (250) 286-6166; 1-888-306-4444 (toll-free)

- Provincial Park and other specialized maps are available from Canadian Cartographics* in Port Coquitlam, BC 1-877-524-3337.

*Carry other BC maps such as 1:20,000 TRIM maps. These and aerial photos can be ordered from the Base Mapping & Geomatic Services Branch, 1st Floor, 810 Blanshard St., Victoria, BC V8W 9M2 (250) 387-6316. For further information visit: http://home.gdbc.gov.bc.ca/catalog or www.landdata.gov.bc.ca

Tidal information is listed in the *Canadian Tide and Current Tables, Vol. 6,* published by the Canadian Hydrographic Service, and available at marine and sporting goods stores.

Other Useful References

Toll-free calling to provincial government offices is available through Enquiry BC (250) 387-6121 or (outside Victoria / within BC) 1-800-663-7867.

BC Ferries

For route and reservation information call (250) 386-3431 (in Victoria / long distance outside of BC) or 1-888-BCFERRY (1-888-223-3779) (in BC / outside the Victoria area); fax (250) 381-5452 or visit: www.bcferries.com.

Ministry of Forests

In 2002, the provincial government, under its Core Review Process, began slashing Ministry of Forests budgets and the servicing of many BC Forest Service recreation sites and roads. By late March 2005, responsibility for BCFS campsites and trails will be transferred to other groups and agencies or cancelled. The requirement for annual recreation site camping passes was eliminated in April 2002 and the BCFS stopped distributing their recreation maps due to potential inaccuracies resulting from the uncertain status of many sites. For BCFS information visit the following websites: www.gov.bc.ca/for/
www.for.gov.bc.ca/hfp/rec/rec.htm (BCFS Recreation Sites)

BC Forest Service, Communications Branch, PO Box 9517, Station Provincial Government, 3rd Floor, 595 Pandora Ave., Victoria, BC V8W 9C3 (250) 387-5255

Campbell River Forest District, 370 South Dogwood St., Campbell River, BC V9W 6Y7 (250) 286-9300

Port McNeill Forest District, PO Box 7000, Port McNeill, BC V0N 2R0 (250) 956-5000

BC Parks

As a result of government cutbacks, information from the former Ministry of Environment, Lands and Parks is available at the following websites:

Ministry of Water, Lands and Air Protection (WLAP):
www.gov.bc.ca/wlap/
http://wlapwww.gov.bc.ca/bcparks/
http://wlapwww.gov.bc.ca/bcparks/index.htm

Ministry of Sustainable Resource Management:
www.gov.bc.ca/srm/
www.bcfisheries.gov.bc.ca/fishinv/fishinfobc.html (Fish Wizard)

BC Parks

4th Floor, 395 Waterfront Crescent, PO Box 9398, Station Provincial
 Government, Victoria, BC V9M 9M9 (250) 387-5002

Note: Park service and maintenance (of the campsites, pit toilets and the
boat launches) will be terminated at selected BC Parks, beginning in April
2002. Other changes include the elimination of interpretive programs, new
firewood fees and altered criteria to qualify for the Disabled Pass Program.
Once the supply of BC Parks brochures (for areas such as Strathcona, Cape
Scott and Clayoquot Sound provincial parks) runs out these pamphlets will
not be reprinted.

Further Information

Boliden (formerly Westmin)
 Myra Falls Operation, PO Box 8000,
 Campbell River, BC V9W 5E2   (250) 287-9271

District of Campbell River
 Leisure Services, 301 St. Ann's Rd.,
 Campbell River, BC V9W 4C7   (250) 923-7911

Regional District of Comox/Strathcona
 350–17th Street, Courtenay, BC V9N 1Y4   (250) 334-6000

Regional District of Mount Waddington
 PO Box 729, Port McNeill, BC V0N 2R0   (250) 956-3301
 www.rdmw.bc.ca

Logging Companies

Canadian Forest Products
 Englewood Division, Woss, BC V0N 3P0   (250) 281-2300

TimberWest
 Beaver Cove Division   (250) 928-3023
 Campbell River Division   (250) 297-9181
 Oyster River Division   (250) 287-7979

Western Forest Products
 Port McNeill Operations   (250) 956-4446
 Holberg Operations   (250) 288-3362

Weyerhaeuser (formerly MacMillan Bloedel)
 North Island Timberlands (incorporates Eve
  River, Kelsey Bay & Menzies Divisions)   (250) 287-5000
 Northwest Bay Division   (250) 468-6810
 Port McNeill Timberlands   (250) 956-5200
 Sproat Lake Operation   (250) 720-4100

Suggested Reading

Akrigg, G.P.V. and Helen B. British Columbia Place Names. Vancouver: UBC Press, (3rd ed.), 1997.

Alberni Environmental Coalition. Alberni Valley Trail Guide. Port Alberni: AEC, 1999.

Baikie, Wallace. Strathcona: a history of British Columbia's first Provincial Park. Campbell River: Ptarmigan Press, 1986.

Baron, Nancy and Acorn, John. Birds of Coastal British Columbia. Vancouver: Lone Pine Publishing, 1997.

Blier, Richard K. More Island Adventures: An Outdoors Guide to Vancouver Island. Victoria: Orca Book Publishers, 1993.

Blier, Richard K. Island Backroads: Hiking, Camping and Paddling on Vancouver Island. Victoria: Orca Book Publishers, 1998.

Blier, Richard K., ed. Hiking Trails II: South-Central Vancouver Island and the Gulf Islands. Victoria: Vancouver Island Trails Information Society, (8th ed.), 2000.

Colbeck, Lynda A. Vancouver Island Shores. Nanaimo: Transcontinental Printing Inc., 1998.

Donaldson-Yarmey, Joan. Backroads of Vancouver Island and the Gulf Islands. Vancouver: Lone Pine Publishing, 1998.

Elms, Lindsay. Beyond Nootka: A Historical Perspective of Vancouver Island Mountains, Courtenay: Misthorn Press, 1996.

Environment Canada. Marine Weather Hazards Manual, West Coast Edition. West Vancouver: Gordon Soules Book Publishing, 1992.

Goldberg, Kim. Where To See Wildlife on Vancouver Island. Madiera Park: Harbour Publishing, 1997.

Graham, Donald. Keepers of the Light. Madiera Park: Harbour Publishing, 1992.

Graham, Donald. Lights of the Inside Passage. Madiera Park, Harbour Publishing, 1992.

Guppy, Walter. Wet Coast Ventures, Mine-Finding on Vancouver Island. Victoria: Cappis Press, 1988.

Guppy, Walter. Clayoquot Soundings: A History of Clayoquot Sound 1880s – 1980s. Tofino: Grassroots Publications, 1997.

Hayman, John. Robert Brown and the Vancouver Island Exploring Expedition. Vancouver: University of British Columbia Press, 1991.

Horvath, Pal. The Nootka Trail: A Backpacker's Guide. (Self-published. See page 172.)

Jones, Elaine. The Northern Gulf Islands Explorer. North Vancouver: Whitecap Books, 1991.

Jones, Laurie. Nootka Sound Explored: A Westcoast History. Campbell River: Ptarmigan Press, 1991.

Kahn, Charles. Hiking the Gulf Islands. Victoria: Orca Book Publishers, 1995.

Lawrence, Susan, ed. Hiking Trails I: Victoria & Vicinity. Victoria: Vancouver Island Trails Information Society, (12th ed.), 1997.

Lebrecht, Sue and Susan Noppe. Adventuring Around Vancouver Island. Vancouver/Toronto: Greystone Books, 1997.

McKnight, George. Sawlogs on Steel Rails. Port Alberni: Port Alberni Seniors' History Committee, 1995.

Meyer, Kathleen. How to Shit In The Woods. Berkeley: Ten Speed Press, 1994.

Nanton, Isabel and Mary Simpson. Adventuring In British Columbia. Vancouver: Douglas & McIntyre, (2nd edition) 1996.

Nicholson, George. Vancouver Island's West Coast 1762-1962. Vancouver: George Nicholson's Books, 1981.

Pacific Yachting, BC Parks and BC Marine Parks Forever Society. BC Marine Parks Guide. Vancouver: Whitecap Books, 1999.

Pacquet, Maggie. Parks of British Columbia and the Yukon. North Vancouver: Maia Publishing, 1990.

Payne, David. Island Cycling: A Cycle Camper's Guide to Vancouver Island. Victoria: Orca Book Publishers, 1996.

Payton, Brian and Bob Herger. Long Beach, Clayoquot and Beyond. Vancouver: Raincoast Books, 1997.

Petersen, Lester R. The Cape Scott Story. Langley: Sunfire, 1985.

Pojar, Jim and Andy Mackinnon. Plants of Coastal British Columbia. Vancouver: Lone Pine Publishing, 1994.

Seagrave, Jayne. Provincial and National Park Campgrounds in BC. Langley: Heritage House, 1997.

Scott, Christine. Nature Campbell River. Courtenay: ABC Printing, 2001.

Sheldon, Ian. Seashore of British Columbia. Vancouver: Lone Pine Publishing, 1998.

Smith, Ian. The Unknown Island. Vancouver: Douglas & McIntyre, 1973.

Stedham, Glen. Bush Basics: A Common Sense Guide to Backwoods Adventure. Victoria: Orca Book Publishers, 1997.

Stoltmann, Randy. Hiking the Ancient Forests of British Columbia and Washington. Vancouver/Edmonton: Lone Pine Publishing, 1996.

Stone, Philip. Island Alpine: A Guide to the Mountains of Strathcona Park and Vancouver Island. Heriot Bay: Wild Isle Publications, 2003.

Taylor, Jeanette and Douglas, Ian. Exploring Quadra Island: Heritage Sites & Hiking Trails. Quathiaski Cove: Fernbank Publishing, 2001.

Thomson, Richard E. Oceanography of the British Columbia Coast. Ottawa: Canadian Special Publication of Fisheries and Aquatic Sciences 56, 1984.

Turner, Robert D. Logging By Rail. Victoria: Sono Nis Press, 1990.

Turner, Robert D. Vancouver Island Railroads. Victoria: Sono Nis Press, 1997.

Walbran, John T., British Columbia Coast Names. Vancouver: Douglas & McIntyre, 1977.

Watmough, Don. Cruising Guide to British Columbia. Vol. IV: West Coast of Vancouver Island, Cape Scott to Sooke. Shoreline: Evergreen Pacific Publications, 1998.

Wild, Paula. Sointula: Island Utopia. Madiera Park: Harbour Publishing, 1995.

(Note: Some of the above are out of print.)

Hiking in Strathcona Provincial Park

In the first edition of this guidebook, published in 1975, the original authors stated, "It is with some misgiving that we publish these details as the high alpine areas can be damaged by over-use and above all by thoughtless camping practices." Their concern was well founded. Today, Strathcona Park is experiencing more use than ever, and some areas are literally being loved to death. Fortunately, most visitors limit themselves to frontcountry areas, where BC Parks' staff have lessened user impact by building trails, designating camping areas, providing toilets and restricting the use of campfires.

The Park Master Plan, developed with a great deal of public input, designates most backcountry areas to "wilderness conservation". While this ensures against floatplanes and helicopters landing there, this category doesn't permit BC Parks to do any maintenance, provide any facilities (including toilets) or even place signs. In fact, these backcountry areas are solely dependent on their isolation for their continued preservation.

This means that if **you** travel a backcountry route, **you alone** bear the responsibility for how much you impact the region. Obviously, this can only work if all hikers passing through ensure they leave no lasting trace. Fortunately, the current climate is towards no-trace camping rather than the bough beds and campfires of the pioneers.

Because each footstep and tent site adds to your impact, backcountry groups should be small in number. At heavily-used locations, such as Forbidden Plateau, Bedwell Lake and the Elk River Trail, you are encouraged to day trip rather than camp unnecessarily overnight.

A concern to preserve Strathcona Park's wilderness experience has led the hiking community to adopt the convention of not building cairns or flagging obvious routes (unless absolutely necessary due to washouts, blowdowns, avalanche debris or logging). Not only are such signs unwelcome evidence of human activity in otherwise pristine places, but leaving such markers may lead others into areas beyond their competence.

James Rutter, January, 1996

Strathcona Park Lodge

Located on the eastern shore of Upper Campbell Lake, 41 km west of Campbell River on Highway 28 to Gold River and 6 km before the road enters Strathcona Provincial Park, this internationally known outdoor recreation centre is well-situated for visitors to this part of the park.

The Lodge offers quality meals and accommodation, and a year-round program for all ages. Instructional courses range from nature walks and canoe camping to white-water kayaking, rock climbing and west coast explorations. The latter include guided hikes along the Nootka Trail. For more information and a free brochure contact: Strathcona Park Lodge, PO Box 2160, Campbell River, BC V9W 5C5 (250) 286-3122 or visit www.strathcona.com

Friends of Strathcona Park (FOSP)

FOSP is a non-profit society with an interest in Strathcona Provincial Park. Stewardship of the park is the key objective of The Friends, and they actively support the management directives described by Strathcona Park's Master Plan. Current activities centre on supporting proposed additions to Strathcona Park, and include discussions with forest industry companies that own land on the park's boundaries. The Friends also sponsor trail-building projects, and have formally "adopted" the Bedwell River Trail.

Strathcona Park Public Advisory Committee (SPPAC)

The Strathcona Park Public Advisory Committee (SPPAC) meets at least twice a year to provide the Environmental Stewardship Regional Manager with advice and strategies for managing Strathcona and Strathcona-Westmin provincial parks. SPPAC (created in 1994) has been very successful and has been used as a model for other provincial advisory groups.

Varied issues include the implementation of the Master Plan and annual modifications, permit applications, public concerns, dwindling provincial funding and specific items referred by the Regional Manager, his staff or the Committee.

Committee members (up to 11 people) possess a broad range of interests, knowledge and expertise that includes a solid understanding of topics relating to Strathcona Provincial Park, aboriginal culture, geology, outdoor recreation, resource management and conservation.

The public are invited to attend SPPAC meetings, which are advertised in local newspapers.

Strathcona Wilderness Institute (SWI)

SWI is a non-profit society, which, through public education, promotes an appreciation and awareness of the natural world – particularly in and around Strathcona Provincial Park on Vancouver Island. SWI operates under a cooperative agreement with BC Parks. The Institute's year-round public education program includes lectures, exhibitions, special events, research projects and publications, as well as educational courses such as Wilderness Self-Reliance, Medicinal Plants, Geology in Strathcona Park, Fall Birding and Coast to Coast Treks.

Interest in creating a Wilderness Institute resulted from a 1992 conference at Strathcona Park Lodge, organized by the FOSP and attended by representatives from forestry, tourism, education and parks sectors. The conference focused on society's relationship to wilderness. What emerged was a resolve to protect existing wilderness areas, along with some methods by which this could be achieved. Based on an agreement that society in general needs to be more knowledgeable about, and more in contact with, the natural world, the Strathcona Wilderness Institute was formed in 1994.

Parts of Strathcona Provincial Park are Important Bird Areas (IBAs), designated sites which provide essential habitat for breeding and non-breeding White-tailed Ptarmigans. Vancouver Island's ptarmigans are a subspecies (*Lagopus leucurus saxatili*) found nowhere else in the world.

The SWI, along with BC Parks, Ministry of WLAP (see page 23), the University of British Columbia, other agencies, various hiking organizations and naturalist clubs, are working to educate the public and create monitoring and research programs. Pending adequate and continued funding, scientific research and volunteer sighting programs will be used in the study of the effects of recreation use and logging on White-tailed Ptarmigan and their fragile habitat.

Sighting cards will be made available at selected trailheads. If you spot a White-tailed Ptarmigan, contact Dr. Kathy Martin, Department of Forest Sciences, UBC, Vancouver, BC V6T 1Z4. (Use the cards if possible.) For more information call the Strathcona Wilderness Institute at (250) 337-1871. **SWI and FOSP**: Box 3404 Courtenay, BC V9N 5N5

Forbidden Plateau: In writing a 1926 article about a visit to the Plateau, Ben Hughes, Editor of the *Comox Argus*, used the name in reference to a diary entry of Dr. Robert Brown, who could not persuade the local natives to accompany him on an exploratory trip up the Puntledge River in 1864. To learn more about the origins of this and other BC geographic names, visit
http://www.gdbc.gov.bc.ca/bcnames

SECTION 1

Access Trails / Routes into Strathcona Park

NOTE: The term "**frontcountry**" refers to regions with serviced camp-sites, usually close to main roads. "**Backcountry**" refers to more remote areas, with wilderness campsites and no amenities.

*The following sub-sections describe in some detail 41 access trails and routes. It is assumed that those travelling these wilderness routes, other than marked trails, are experienced hikers or climbers competent at map reading and route finding, and equipped with map, compass and altimeter. Many hikers also carry a GPS. It is important that you read the preceding section, **Hiking in Strathcona Park,** page 28; **How To Use This Book,** page 14; and **Hints and Cautions**, page 15, before reading further.*

*A Core Area Camping Zone exists for Forbidden Plateau. **Backcountry Fee Collection Zones and Designated Camping Areas** apply to the Bedwell Lake / Price Creek corridor and the Elk River Trail. Metal food caches are in place at all Forbidden Plateau campsites. The hanging caches have been removed.*

*Currently, **no fires are allowed** in the Bedwell Lake / Price Creek corridor and Forbidden Plateau's core area. Starting in 2003, **campfires will be prohibited anywhere in the backcountry** of Strathcona Provincial Park, including the Elk River Valley. Fires will be permitted at designated fire rings at high-use campgrounds (such as the Buttle Lake and Ralph River campsites on Buttle Lake) and various marine sites.*

No camping is allowed within one kilometre of any road. BC Parks dis-courages the marking of routes by any means. The use of paint or other permanent markers is illegal. Off-road horse riding and bicycling are not allowed anywhere in Strathcona Park and a penalty fine is in place for vio-lations

COMOX GLACIER

Trails in the Forbidden Plateau and Comox Glacier Areas

Special thanks to Ruth Masters for her Forbidden Plateau updates and Ken Rodonets and Lindsay Elms for their Comox Lake reports.

Two public roads lead to Forbidden Plateau, namely, the road to Wood Mountain Provincial Ski Park (site of the burned-down Plateau Ski Lodge), and the now-paved Mount Washington (Strathcona Parkway) Road to the Mount Washington Ski Resort. and Paradise Meadows. Both routes are accessed from the Inland Island Highway (Highway 19).

For the **Wood Mountain**[i] access to Forbidden Plateau, from Highway 19 take Exit 127 to Piercy Road and turn right. Forbidden Plateau Road passes **Nymph Falls Regional District Park (55.5 ha)**, on the Puntledge River. Here you'll discover trails for both hikers and mountain bikers. In the spring of 2002, the Outdoor Recreation Council of BC named the **Puntledge River**[ii] to a list of BC's second-most-endangered steelhead rivers.

The **Mount Washington**[iii] turn is 10 km north of Exit 127. Logging roads (other than Weyerhaeuser's road to Norm Lake used to access Gem Lake Trail) are administered by TimberWest. Call ahead for current access restrictions. Extreme fire hazard may restrict entry. Many roads in the Comox Lake region have been improved. The **Divers**[iv]/**Rossiter**[v] **lakes area (1027 ha)**, near the headwaters of the Oyster River, was slated to be added to Forbidden Plateau in 2002, to protect old-growth yellow cedar.

The Forbidden Plateau trails are long-established and offer opportunities for day or overnight hiking. The Comox District Mountaineering Club (CDMC) and BC Parks have erected signs on trees at trail junctions. Remember that trails can become hard to follow in this unique alpine area and it is easy to take a wrong fork. When fog sets in trails can become

---

i   **Wood Mountain:** The Clinton S. Wood family built the Plateau Lodge, 1933-34. It burned down in July, 1982. (Stuart Wood Island in Moat Lake is named for the eldest son, killed in W.W. II.)

ii **Puntledge River:** Dr. Brown named the river after a now-extinct Salish clan who lived along its banks. Meaning "buried belly", the name has also been rendered as "Pentlatch" and "Puntluch".

iii **Mount Washington:** Captain Richards named the mountain after Rear Admiral John Washington of the British Navy, who was Secretary of the Royal Geographical Society for many years and who succeeded Sir Francis Beaufort as Hydrographer in 1855.

iv **Divers Lake:** The name comes from the loons ("hell-divers") who inhabit the lake.

v   **Rossiter Lake:** Len Rossiter was an early guide to Forbidden Plateau.

---

confusing, and maps and compass will be essential. **Note:** Should horse riders or mountain bikers be encountered off-road, hikers should consider that tourists may have unwittingly made a mistake, and inform them politely. Other abusers should be reported to BC Parks staff. Pets must be leashed at all times.

Owing to increased recreational use and its resulting impact in the Plateau area, low-impact camping techniques are very important, with an emphasis on good sanitary habits and effective waste management. BC Parks has provided pit toilets at various locations. Elsewhere, defecate in the bush well away from streams. Carry a plastic trowel so you can dig a small scat hole, and either flame your toilet paper or pack it out with you in a plastic bag (because it won't decompose). This is important. Take out **all** garbage.

Due to a concern over depletion of Forbidden Plateau's natural resources, BC Parks has designated a core area within which camping is restricted to specific, hardened sites and no fires are permitted. Starting in 2003, no campfires will be permitted in the backcountry of Strathcona Park; camp stoves are the essential alternative. In the core area camping is permitted only at **Kwai Lake,**[i] **Circlet Lake**[ii] and **Lake Helen Mackenzie,** and these sites have pit toilets. Outside the core area there is camping at **Douglas**[iii] and **McKenzie**[iv] lakes but no toilets, and BC Parks has no immediate plans to put any in. **Fees for camping in the core area are $5 per person (16 years and older), per night (2002).**

Useful reference material:

The BC Parks' pamphlet on Strathcona Provincial Park provides much useful information. Obtain a copy soon at local tourist infocentres and some sporting goods stores. When the current supply is exhausted these informative brochures will not be reprinted. (See *BC Parks* on page 23.) *Maps of the Comox Valley*, published by Comox Valley Ground Search and Rescue Association, covers the Forbidden Plateau and Comox Lake areas. (See *Map Sources,* page 21-22.)

---

i   *Kwai* means "wood" in the local native language. This multi-lingual pun refers to the C.S. Wood family, who pioneered the camps and trails on Forbidden Plateau.

ii   **Circlet Lake:** This round lake was originally named Circle Lake by John Brown, a 1920s black prospector. The name was changed in 1939 to avoid duplication within BC. The lake lies within a cirque, so the name is doubly apt.

iii   **Douglas Lake:** William (Bill) Douglas was a Courtenay alderman and he carried the fry in to stock Douglas and McKenzie lakes with trout. Ruth Masters notes that he is "remembered by all who were children in the 1930s, since he bought cascara bark and beer bottles, our only source of income."

iv   **McKenzie Lake:** John McKenzie was mayor of Courtenay at the time when water rights were obtained and a dam built in 1929.

(a) Mount Becher Trail (Map E3)

The Mount Becher Trail is a great choice for a day hike. A good, well-defined trail leads from the site of the burnt-out Plateau Ski Lodge (razed by vandals in 2002) to **Mount Becher**[i].

From Courtenay, drive on public roads to the Plateau Ski Lodge parking area, about 19 km. It's about 9 km from the trailhead to Mount Becher and back. More experienced hikers can head back from **Mount Becher (1385 m)** following a rugged, sometimes hard-to-locate route via the **Boston Ridge**[ii]. (Looping back this way adds 4 km to your hike.) There are some marvellous views. The route is fairly steep in places, particularly where it drops from the ridge to Boston Creek and the Boston Main logging road. Continue along an old rail grade back up to the Plateau road, at a switchback, just below the lodge site. This route was originally constructed and flagged by CDMC.

(b) Paradise Meadows Access (Map D2)

Take the Mount Washington Road (also called the Strathcona Parkway) from Highway 19 and follow the signs to the ski resort. Turn left onto the road to the Nordic lodge and continue another 1.5 km to the parking area. From Courtenay to the Nordic ski parking lot and start of trail is about 25 km. The BC Parks pamphlet detailing the trails on Forbidden Plateau is no longer available.

(c) Paradise Meadows Loop (Map D2)

This trail starts at Mount Washington's Nordic ski parking lot and runs down to the brown bridge on the old Battleship Lake Trail, then returns on the other side of Paradise Creek - length 2.2 km. It is a beautiful walk suitable for all ages. The trail is mostly boardwalk.

(d) Helen Mackenzie Loop Trail (Map D2)

This 2.9 km trail from **Paradise Meadows**[iii] winds gently through rolling meadows to bring walkers of almost any level of ability to **Lake Helen**

---

i   Becher Bay, near Victoria, and **Mount Becher** are named after Captain Alexander Bridport Becher (1796-1876), a respected surveying officer of the Royal Navy.

ii **Boston Creek, Lake, and Ridge:** E.J. "Boston" Calman (who had once lived in Boston), of "Happy Valley" near Cumberland, had a cabin at Boston Bay on Comox Lake when he was a young man.

iii **Paradise Meadows:** Named by C.S. Wood when he was exploring for the Dove Creek Trail in 1928.

Mackenzie[i]. Following the lakeshore trail eastwards (ie. to the left) leads to the west side of Battleship Lake where you join the main trail back to Paradise Meadows. This pleasant loop requires about three hours, not including rest stops.

At Lake Helen Mackenzie there's a well-developed campsite that is suitable for people who arrive late on their journey into the park, for first-time backcountry campers, or for those with small children looking for a backcountry experience. Core area camping fees apply.

(e) Kwai Lake Loop Trail (Map D2)

At Lake Helen Mackenzie turn west to follow a rough but easy grade trail which ascends to subalpine meadows near the Park Rangers' cabin, and your first good views of **Mount Albert Edward** and **Mount Regan**[ii]. Turn left at **Hairtrigger Lake**[iii] and pass **Kwai Lake** on your left, a very beautiful and rewarding destination. Kwai is the second campsite in the core area, also well developed with tent pads, toilets and food caches. Core area camping fees apply. To return, follow signs to **Croteau Lake**[iv], and from there to **Battleship Lake**[v]. This 15 km loop requires a full day.

(f) Mount Albert Edward Trail/Route (Map D2)

From the Rangers' cabin (see (e), above) maintain your elevation to pass Hairtrigger Lake on your left. Another hour brings you to a short side trail leading to Circlet Lake. A developed campsite exists at this popular location and it is a good place to stop before a steep climb onto the ridge leading to Albert Edward - especially with full packs. The trail becomes a route after the shoulder and tarns (small mountain lakes) at 1400 m. The summit (2094 m elevation) is about six hours from the parking lot, one way. Many groups camp at Circlet Lake and travel light for a summit day-return (6 km and four hours one way). Remember to pack for a long day, and carry what you will need for exposed ridge travel and sudden weather changes.

---

i   **Lake Helen Mackenzie:** Helen assisted her uncle, Lt. Gov. Randolf Bruce, when he formally opened the Dove Creek Trail in 1929.

ii   **Mount Regan:** Mr. Regan, a CPR surveyor, named the mountain after himself in 1930.

iii **Hairtrigger Lake:** Clinton Wood named the lake after he pulled the trigger too soon and missed his shot at a deer.

iv   **Croteau Lake:** Eugene Croteau of Croteau Beach, Comox, established Croteau Camp after the Dove Creek Trail opened. Guests could tent at sites on the lakeside and take their meals in the central cabin with cooking and dining facilities.

v   **Battleship Lake** was named by Clinton Wood after his son observed that the outlines of the trees on the lake's three small islands resemble battleships.

(g) Gem Lake Trail   (Map D2)

There is restricted access on the logging road up Oyster River to **Norm Lake**[i]. A staffed security gate at Mile 16 ensures the road is closed to the public until 5 pm weekdays. It is open throughout weekends. Check with Weyerhaeuser's office in Campbell River. (See *Logging Companies* on page 24.) From Norm Lake, a trail follows the grown-in road up to Gem Creek, then the west side of the creek to **Gem Lake**[ii]. This trail was constructed and marked to Gem Lake by CDMC.

(h) Sunrise Lake[iii] Route   (Map D2)

Just south of the Oyster River bridge, turn off the Duncan Bay Main onto Oyster River Main. (Note: this is not the same road as Weyerhaeuser's Oyster River Main on the north side of the river.) Head southwest for roughly 10 km and turn right onto Rossiter Main for 5 km to a bridge over **Piggott Creek**[iv] (Branch 151-5). After the bridge, pass through a gate, which is locked on weekdays, but should be unlocked on weekends. Check with TimberWest's Oyster River Division and be careful not to get locked in when crews go home. (See *Logging Companies* on page 24.) Turn north across a bridge over Harris Creek. Stay on the west side of this creek to road's end (8 km) just west of the outfall of Harris Lake[v]. Cross the creek to the start of the route.

Comox Lake Area Access:
Extensive helicopter logging has taken place in the Comox Lake area in recent years and is ongoing. Some trails and routes have been affected by clearcuts. TimberWest and the CDMC have worked together to re-route, clear and re-establish many of the region's popular trails. Roads have been improved, but they are still narrow and winding. There are some steep hills. TimberWest hauls along area mainlines and public access is usually restricted to weekends and holidays only, or after 6 pm on weekdays. You have to check in at the watchman's security station, just up the road from the dam at the foot of Comox Lake. There are currently no entry fees charged. Before your hike call TimberWest's Oyster River Division for current information.

---

i   **Norm Lake:** N.C. (Norm) Stewart, BCLS, did the detailed serial topographical map of the Forbidden Plateau area, 1934-35, and named many of its features.

ii   **Gem Lake:** Originally named "Emerald Lake" by the Regan (E&N) Survey Party in 1930, but changed to eliminate duplication.

iii   **Sunrise Lake:** C.S. Wood camped above this lake in 1928 and watched the sun rise over the lake.

iv   **Piggott Creek:** Julian A. Piggott was Helen Mackenzie's fiance.

v   **Harris Lake and Creek** are named after a trapper who lived in Courtenay.

(See *Logging Companies* on page 24.) The TimberWest logging road map for this region is no longer available.

(i) Alone Mountain Trail (Map E4)

This makes a nice spring hike since the snow goes off the southern slope a few weeks earlier than on other mountains. From the causeway and dam at the foot of Comox Lake, drive approximately 13.5 km along TimberWest's Comox Lake Main to just before the top of the hill near the Cruickshank River bridge. Watch for a sign saying "Heliport 15 and Alone Mountain Trail". A very short logging road leads in toward **Alone Mountain**[i]. At its end look for a big hole, on the right, where a large boulder has been removed. Blue paint and an arrow indicate the start of the trail. Follow the trail north up to the top of **Alone Mountain (847 m)**. In clear weather there are good views of Comox Glacier. The spring flowers are always beautiful and there are wild onions for nibbling. This trail was built and marked by CDMC.

(j) Idiens/Capes Lakes Route (Maps E4, D3 and D4)

From the causeway and dam at the foot of Comox Lake, take Comox Lake Main for 14.5 km to the **Cruickshank River**[ii] bridge. On the south side of the river, swing right, down to the river and follow Cruickshank Main approximately 3 km to South Main[35]. Turn left (south) onto South Main for 0.5 km to a large, cleared log sorting area, on the right. The trail begins in the southwest corner, near an old logging road. There is no longer any vehicle access up this steep spur, so park at the bottom.

At first the trail follows the original route part way up the old logging road until it reaches a bench overlooking Comox Creek and the Cruickshank River. Instead of following the old road at this point and going up the east side of the slope, it now continues straight ahead and climbs, via several switchbacks, up the south side of the slope, through a stand of trees. The trail is well designated, with flagging tape and a series of blue paint marks.

Watch for a sign pointing to Idiens Lake, where there is good swimming in hot weather. Blazes lead to the Idiens Lake[iii] memorial cairn. The route leads around the south side of Idiens Lake to Lee Plateau, where camping

---

i   **Alone Mountain:** Formerly "Lone Mountain", the name was changed to eliminate duplication.

ii   **Cruickshank River:** George Cruickshank was Honourable Secretary of the committee that initiated the Vancouver Island Exploration Expedition of 1864.

iii   **Idiens Lake:** Richard Bertram "Dick" Idiens was an ardent hiker, skier and early president of the CDMC, who was killed during W.W. II. The name was proposed by Ruth Masters, adopted in 1964, and a cairn was erected in 1965.

is possible and an excellent view of Comox Glacier is provided. Continue south down to **Capes Creek**[i], avoiding the few cliffs. The Capes memorial cairn and plaque are just before the outfall of Capes Creek. From Capes Creek go roughly southeast up to Capes Ridge, where you get the most magnificent view of Comox Glacier. Return via Capes Lake, branching right directly to the Idiens / Capes Lakes junction and then out the way you came in. Allow five hours, one way, for the ascent.

Even though the end of Capes Ridge shows on the map as being near South Main road, it is a precarious trip down, with huge belts of cliffs which are nearly impossible to avoid, and this method of return is definitely not recommended.

(k) Century Sam Lake Trail   (Maps E4 and D4)

From the causeway and dam at the foot of Comox Lake, take TimberWest's Comox Lake Main, then Cruickshank Main, about 17.5 km to the junction with South Main.[35] Cut left and take South Main approximately 7 km to a junction where the road to **Cougar Lake**[ii] swings off to the left (southeast). Keep right (northwest) for about 2 km to **Datsio**[iii] **Creek**.[34] There is no further vehicle access beyond this point as the road has deteriorated and there are numerous washouts. Park on the side of the road and make sure you leave room for others to turn around. Hike to the end of the logging road and the log crossing for the Comox Glacier Trail.[36]

This low-elevation trail to **Century Sam Lake**[iv] starts just west of the log crossing [36] for Comox Glacier Trail and goes up the south side of Comox Creek to the lake and a nice little campsite. The trail, made by CDMC in the 1960s, is brushed out seasonally. Expect windfall in the upper section below the lake after winter. The trail can be difficult to find at the bottom of the avalanche paths when the bushes are thick over the summer.

---

i   According to Karl Stevenson in his *Hiking in Strathcona Park* (1974), Geoff **Capes** was an early hiker who missed being the first to climb the Golden Hinde by one day, being bested by N.C. Stewart, the surveyor.

ii   **Cougar Lake:** In this case, the lake is named after the nearby "Cougar Main" logging road of the Comox Logging Co. whereas Panther Lake was named by John Brown, who told of encountering a family of cougars who chased him up a tree.

cougar tracks

iii   **Datsio Creek:** This name, native for "a native person", was bestowed by N.C. Stewart (see Norm Lake).

iv   **Century Sam Lake:** Sid Williams of Courtenay was a hiker, climber and prospector in these parts; he also played the part of Century Sam during the 1958 Centennial Celebrations. The lake was named in 1961, and a memorial cairn has been built.

The trail winds along Comox Creek's south side to the bottom of the first avalanche slide path. Thick spring vegetation can make the route here hard to see. The trail angles up slightly and enters the forest again and then into a second slide area. The trail angles up again into the trees and out into a third avalanche slide area. Next comes a steep ascent into the forest and a section of windfall. The trail eventually emerges at the river just below Century Sam Lake where there are some rough campsites and a memorial cairn to Sid Williams.

(I) Comox Glacier Trail/Route (Maps E4 and D4)

Ropes are essential equipment when traversing icefields and active glaciers such as the Comox and Cliffe glaciers. While crevasses for the most part are obvious, in the spring or after a snowfall, they may be thinly covered and hazardous to both the uninitiated and the experienced. Just look at the worldwide statistics for the number of people falling into crevasses unroped. There have been small accidents on Comox[i] Glacier, but no crevasse fatalities, as yet. Be prepared and ultra-cautious.

This trip is only for strong hikers and should be made in reasonable weather. It's a good three-day hike: one day to the "frog pond" campsite, about 1.5 km along the ridge; a second day to travel light, up to the glacier and back to camp; and a third day to pack out. (*See Comox Lake Area Access* on page 36.)

As above for the Century Sam Lake Trail, take TimberWest's Comox Lake Main (from the causeway and dam at the foot of Comox Lake), then Cruickshank Main to the South Main junction.[35] Follow South Main for around 7 km and keep right (northwest) at the Cougar Lake turn and continue to the parking area at Datsio Creek[34] where the bridge here has been pulled. Beyond this point the road is washed out. Remember to leave space for others to turn around. You can seasonally make the journey in a two-wheel-drive vehicle. It's a 2.5 km hike along the logging road to the start of the trail.[36]

From here, take the log crossing to a section of trail with switchbacks. Unfortunately this only goes about a quarter of the way up and there is a lot of work to do to gain the ridge. About a kilometre along the ridge there is a saddle[ii] which the hiker must negotiate. Descend from the ridge on the

---

i   **Comox:** This is a shortened form of the word for "abundance" (referring to plenty of game and berries) in the Yaculta (Euclataw) dialect.

ii   a **saddle**, or **col**, is a depression between two summits

south side. The route is steep and exposed and there is loose rock. The distance from the saddle to the frog ponds is not far.

After the frog ponds, the trail becomes a rough route and in places the rock steps can be quite intimidating, especially to tired hikers. This is a good place to use a rope for assurance, and you are advised to carry one (you should have one for the glacier anyway). There is also a lack of available water on this section.

There is a steep ascent to the ridge at the 1240 m level, which leads to **Black Cat Mountain**[i] (the access ridge has fine views of Comox Glacier and of Century Sam Lake below). Follow along, up and over the north shoulder of Black Cat Mountain, down to **Lone Tree Pass**[ii]. It's a direct scramble from here up to the south end of Comox Glacier. Cross a wide flat snowfield to a cairn. Get out if fog closes in, and be able to use map and compass to cross the glacier to the trailhead.

Backpacking gear is required, also maps and compass. Ice axes and ropes are crucial. Pack a portable stove for cooking, as fires will be restricted in the park's backcountry as of 2003. No-impact camping is a preferable goal. See connecting routes on Map D4 of this book. The trail was built and marked by CDMC in the early 1960s.

(m) Kookjai Mountain Route to Comox Glacier
(Maps E4, E5 and D4)

Though a longer access to Comox Glacier, the **Kookjai Mountain**[iii] route crosses a lovely plateau area and avoids having to negotiate the exposed rock sections of the frog pond route. Drive in from the foot of Comox Lake as described above but keep left (southeast) at the Cougar Lake turn on South Main. Pull your vehicle off the road about 400 or 500 m north of where the logging road turns sharply to the east [46] on its way to **Rough and Tumble Mountain**[iv].

Heft your pack for an ascent of the obvious ridge to the west, perhaps skirting some bluffs at the 600 m level depending on the line you take. Follow

---

i   **Black Cat Mountain**: Back in the '20s a hiking group was heading out of Courtenay in foul weather when a black cat ran across their path. As they climbed, the weather cleared, which was light-heartedly attributed to the cat's earlier appearance.

ii **Lone Tree Pass:** One lone tree is visible in the pass between Black Cat Mountain and the Comox Glacier.

iii **Kookjai Mountain:** Norm Stewart applied a local word for "to see", this being the first place from which one can see the Comox Glacier en route from Comox Gap.

iv **Rough and Tumble Mountain:** This is another one of Norm Stewart's names.

the backbone of the ridge right up above the tree line. The going is good once you reach old-growth timber, but before that you will have a punishing bush-bash of two or three hours.

Tatsno[i] Lakes [47] is a very beautiful location with good tent sites and views. If you have more time, then **Kwassun Lake[ii]** is another good camping place, with good access to clean water and it's perhaps less "buggy" than the Tatsno Lakes. From here it is possible to day trip to Comox Glacier following a system of ridges leading to Black Cat Mountain, where you join the Comox Glacier Route (above) at Lone Tree Pass. This makes for a very long trek, so if you can go further on your first day you will shorten your second.

The route from **Kookjai Mountain (1279 m)** to the base of Black Cat Mountain is easy and well defined with numerous tarns and places to camp. A good (low-impact) camp can be made at 1400 m, up on the ridge summit, west of Tatsno Lakes. Shortly after beginning the climb up Black Cat Mountain there are bluffs that turn to the right and then it is necessary to zigzag through further bluffs to the alpine. It is easy from there to reach the top and Lone Tree Pass. It can be tricky finding your way back down through the bluffs on Black Cat Mountain towards Kookjai Mountain.

Oshinow Lake Area

This area, which has been heavily logged, includes the most southeasterly portion of Strathcona Provincial Park. The south end of **Oshinow Lake[iii]** is accessed from Elsie Lake via a gravel mainline (which is seasonally suitable for high-clearance two-wheel-drive vehicles) that climbs the Ash River Valley. Elsie Lake, in turn, is reached from Courtenay to the north (on TimberWest roads) by way of Comox Lake (see *Comox Lake Area Access* on page 36) and from Port Alberni to the southeast (on Weyerhaeuser roads).

Access may be restricted due to active logging or high forest fire hazard. Road conditions are subject to change due to flooding, erosion, washouts and slowdown. Horses and mountain bikes are permitted on the older logging roads in this area.

---

i   **Tatsno Lakes:** the source of this name is unknown, although Allan C. Brooks surmises that it could be a variation of *Datsio*.

ii **Kwassun Lake:** The name means "star" in the local dialect.

iii **Oshinow Lake:** The name is from the local word meaning "all kinds of game".

Rugged mountains border Willemar Lake.

(a) Upper Puntledge Route via Willemar Lake
(Maps E5 and D4)

Parts of this region have been clearcut and heli-logging was prevalent in early 2002. A new logging road extends around Willemar Lake and along the Forbush Lakes. Future logging could impact hiking routes in this area. There is restricted public access on TimberWest logging roads along Comox Lake. (See *Comox Lake Area Access* on page 36.)

You will need a canoe for this. Drive on TimberWest logging roads past the south end of Comox Lake to the foot of **Willemar Lake**[i]. Paddle to the top end of Willemar and drag your canoe up the channel (about 200 m) or take the portage trail on the left. ("It's right where you need it," says Ruth Masters, who helped put it in). Re-launch for a short (under a kilometre) paddle through an "everglades" marshy area leading into **Forbush Lake**[ii].

The best camping place is at the top of the lake on the remains of an old cat-logging road that stopped at the Park boundary. Continue hiking on this old road, which has now softened into a pleasant trail, into the magnificent old-growth forest of the Upper Puntledge. After about 2 km there is a delightful rest spot at a waterfall. From there on, the trail has been allowed to grow over, though it is a reasonable route through open timber all the way to Puntledge Lake. From here there are feasible and challenging route possibilities to the Ash River and over to Drinkwater Creek, as well as connections to Margaret Lake and out by way of Price Creek.

(b) Oshinow Lake Access   (MAPS E5 and D5)

Camping and vehicle access is possible on the lakeshore, just north of the creek that drains into Oshinow Lake from Toy Lake. This is a feasible boat launch. The old logging road on the northeast side of Oshinow Lake is suitable only for mountain bikes or hiking.

(c) Toy, Junior and June Lakes Access   (Map E5)

From Oshinow Lake you can hike a few kilometres northeast along the logging road to three small lakes. June Lake is adjacent to the road. At Junior Lake a small trail along the old road leads 200 m to the lakeshore. Another short spur road goes right to Toy Lake.

---

i   **Willemar Lake:** The Reverend J.X. Willemar was the first Roman Catholic priest in Comox District.

ii **Forbush Lake**: Edward Howe Forbush was an ornithologist who collected specimens in Comox District. (Willemar and Forbush lakes used to be known as The Little Lakes.)

Della Falls Trail
(Maps D5 and C5)

This area is remote and requires water travel down Great Central Lake, one of Vancouver Island's longest lakes (over 35 km long, with a surface area of 5085 ha). Watch for bears. Beware of avalanches in the winter and early spring. Following severe winters, lingering snows block the trail well into June in the upper valley. Flooding and high water may delay or prevent passage. The trail is seasonally overgrown and hard to find in some areas. Parts of the route up the Drinkwater Valley above Della Falls are extremely difficult.

The Della Falls Trail leads hikers from the head of Great Central Lake to the base of Canada's highest falls (440 m), a cascade that tumbles down from Della Lake. This 16 km trail, by way of Drinkwater Creek, is a long hike (about seven hours, one way) suitable for intermediate level hikers. The trail was originally built by Joe Drinkwater, a trapper and area miner. He also started the Ark Resort. **Della Falls** is named after his wife.[i]

For Great Central Lake take Highway 4 west from Port Alberni for just under 10 km and turn right (north) onto Great Central Lake Road. Continue another 7.5 km to the Ark Resort. You can park here for a small fee and rent or launch a boat or canoe for your journey to the Della Falls trailhead, at the head of Great Central Lake. Allow three days for a round trip if using a powerboat and six days by canoe.

A second lake access point is situated part way down the lake's north side. As above, drive to Great Central Lake and just before reaching the Ark Resort turn right (north) onto Weyerhaeuser's Ash River Main and cross the logging road bridge. These roads are administered by Weyerhaeuser's Sproat Operation. Call ahead to check on current access restrictions. (See *Logging Companies* on page 24.)

After about 6.5 km turn left (west) onto Branch 83. Stay on Branch 83 for 9.3 km to a road intersection, south of Lowry Lake. Turn left (south) on a secondary spur and continue about 1.5 km to the BCFS Scout Beach Recreation Site and boat launch. From here a trail, 2.5 km in length, follows up a wide valley to Lowry Lake where there is great fishing. From the lakeshore camping area, just southeast of the BC Hydro facility, canoeing time to the head of the Great Central Lake is about four or five hours.

---

[i]   **Margaret Lake** is named after Lady McBride. Sir Richard McBride was premier of BC when Strathcona Park was created in 1911.

Returning from a hike to Della Falls, canoeists take advantage of the winds on Great Central Lake.

The north and south shores of this long, narrow lake are very precipitous, so if canoeing or kayaking, get an early morning start. The lake is usually windswept by west winds in mid-afternoon and the water can be very rough with whitecaps. Watch for deadheads and standing dead trees along the shore, due to the raising of the lake level. In case of rough water, follow the shoreline despite the hazards. There are a few possible campsites about halfway along the north shore; those along the south shore are a little better.

Route Description:
Map D5
The Della Falls Trail starts at the head of Great Central Lake, on the lake's east shore. (The nearby **McBride Creek addition (3750 ha)** expands Strathcona Provincial Park's southern boundary.) At the Della Falls trailhead BC Parks has developed a camping area with a bear-proof cache, a pit toilet and a canoe/kayak rack. There is a collection station here but currently (2002) no fees are being charged. Along the trail, all the suspension bridges have been replaced with timber bridges and a steel one. Much of the trail follows an old roadbed left behind from the days of logging and mining early in this century. The first 7 km follows the flats through a mixed second-growth forest to Margaret Creek. Once across the bridge at this creek the trail continues through some old-growth forest for 4 km, gently gaining elevation.

Map C5
About 11 km up the valley a bridge over a scenic gorge crosses Drinkwater Creek. From there the trail gets rougher and climbs to a second bridge at the 12.5 km point. These spans are sometimes washed out or crushed or damaged by fallen trees. Take care at all creek traverses. Beyond the second crossing a challenging section of the route passes through a rockslide which pushes you close to the creek. Gaining elevation again the trail leads up to the **Love Lake Trail / Mount Septimus**[i] junction at about the 15 km mark. The last kilometre to Della Falls emerges from open old growth forest into an avalanche run-out zone near the base of the falls. Della Falls has three successive drops, each about 150 m in height. A climb to the top of the falls is possible but a little dangerous.

Summer work crews have sporadically improved and brushed out the trail up to the falls and built several bridges. In 2001 BC Parks replaced three bridges that had been badly damaged by the severe snows of 1998. Check maps **C5** and **D5** for campsites and toilets (toilet paper is not supplied). **BC Parks strongly advises visitors not to camp near the old sawmill site,**

---

i   **Mount Septimus:** Septimus Evans was surgeon on the SS *Beaver.* By happy coincidence, the mountain has seven peaks.

about one kilometre below the falls. This area is surrounded by decadent forest (the trees are decaying and subject to blowdown) and is not suitable for camping. Instead find an alternate location along the creek's north side (dependent on water levels) that is not situated under any large or hazardous trees. When camping anywhere along Drinkwater Creek, be aware that the water can rise suddenly.

On the hike in, you can also camp on the Drinkwater Creek gravel bar, about 2 km before the Love Lake turn-off. The building of campfires will be prohibited in Strathcona Park's backcounty as of 2003. Use a portable backpacking stove instead. There is much evidence of the extensive mining activity in the Della Falls area. Please do not remove or destroy any remaining equipment or relics, which now form part of the historical record.

(a) To Della Lake

Experienced climbers can tackle a difficult and dangerous route that leads up the cliffs to the south of the falls. To get there, cross the Drinkwater Creek on the main bridge just above the upper campsite area. Walk 100 m and look for an overgrown trail to the left. The correct route to Della Lake crosses a single-beam bridge, 25 m after leaving the trail to the falls. The route takes you up through dense bush to the base of cliffs and then it follows obvious lines up through steep mixed ground. Above 800 m it leads up and right [44], through bush, and connects to a ledge. This ledge leads up cliffs and straightforward ramps to Della Lake, which is in a spectacular setting of rugged mountain peaks.

Della Falls – Canada's highest waterfall.

(b) To Love Lake

Our map shows the switchbacking trail, starting by the old sawmill site, which goes up to Love Lake. Turn uphill at the sign "Love Lake / Mount Septimus". This is now a well-built trail and a pleasant hike to good (best at 1200 m level) views of Della Falls. The trail switchbacks steeply. At the 1220 m level, break off to the right and pick up the trail to Love Lake. See also Section 2, routes (c), page 72, and (i), page 83.

Note: The Ark Resort rents out canoes and powerboats. Ask for the Della Falls special rate, which currently (2002) includes a four-day canoe rental for $60/person or a three-day power boat rental for the same price, plus fuel. You can also camp at the Ark Resort. They have 20 campsites for $17/night (and nine RV sites). For information contact the resort at (250) 723-2657 or visit www.arkresort.com.

Bedwell River (Oinimitis) Trail
(Maps B6, B5 and C5)

The Bedwell[i] River Trail has received little maintenance or upgrading in recent years. Because of bad weather and a lack of funds and support, the 2001 trail-clearing effort, by the Friends of Strathcona Park (FOSP), went only as far as K2 Creek, below Oinimitis Lake. The route is overgrown in places and difficult to find (particularly in the Ashwood Creek area and the lower valley where salmonberry and elderberry thrive) and many sections have eroded along the riverbank. The old road has washed out in several spots and the decayed bridges are now completely gone. That means more river crossings. These areas may be treacherous or impassable in times of wet weather and high water. Several slide areas, some the result of logging, impede the route.

The Bear River was the traditional home of the Oinimitis (meaning "bear") people, who, in the fall, would gather at the delta to fish and hunt. In 1865, John Buttle travelled up this river, climbing an unnamed mountain near Ursus Creek to discover Buttle Lake in the Island's interior. (*Ursus* is Latin for "bear".) He was soon followed by placer miners who swarmed here on the rumour of gold. Mining has continued in this valley since that time, and in 1962 the lower valley was partially logged. In the winter of 1994/95 the first 2 km of the old logging road were re-opened and an area

---

i **Bedwell Sound:** Captain Richards, in command of the early surveying vessels on the coast, named Bedwell Sound after Edward Parker Bedwell, second master of HM Surveying Vessel *Plumper*, 1857-1860. The name Bedwell then came to be applied to the river and lake as well.

of privately-owned timber was clearcut. The valley has been deleted from, and returned to, Strathcona Park since 1986. The Oinimitis Trail was built by the Friends of Strathcona to provide access to this remote and delightful valley.

Approach: From Tofino, boat or air transportation is needed to reach the head of Bedwell Sound, approximately 32 km. If you're travelling by sea kayak or canoe, this trip will take about a day and a half. Powerboat transportation can be arranged through The Whale Centre in Tofino and the trip takes about 1.5 hours.

Trail Head: The trail begins at an obvious, open flat area by the logging road bridge but fill up your water jugs before you land there because there is no fresh water close to the trailhead. Respect the private land in this area.

Map B6

Trail Description: From the landing area, follow the logging road north, through 2 km of logged forest to reach the first camping site and fresh water, near the confluence of Ursus Creek. From this point the trail follows the banks of the Bedwell River and there are good views of Ursus Mountain. One kilometre farther on, cross **Cotter Creek[i]** and then, just past Penny Creek, a small trail to the right leads to Walter Guppy's riverside cabin (about 4 km from tidewater). This is a good shelter in bad weather.

The main trail begins to climb a little and you reach the "3-Mile" log-crossing [40], where the trail crosses above a gorge on the Bedwell River. Here a fine suspension bridge has been constructed by the FOSP. In August, 1994, the FOSP dedicated this bridge to Gayle McGee, a departed Friend and enviro/activist.

One kilometre north you reach the unmarked boundary of Strathcona Park. The trail now opens up and stays well above the main river-canyon. There are beautiful deep pools and water-carved rocks where the river bends (well below the trail), and a fine view of Mariner Mountain.

After the rock-cut, the trail becomes narrower, and after 500 m leads you to a rocky washout which can be tricky to cross. Shortly after this the Bedwell River is again crossed, this time via an overgrown bridge, high above a narrow canyon where the river roars far below. This is an interesting viewing point!

Map B5

Approximately 800 m farther on, several flagging tapes on the left mark the beginning of the difficult route [41] to **Mariner Mountain (1785 m)**. This

---

i   **Cotter Creek:** Named after an official of Abco Mines.

route is quite steep, and should only be attempted by experienced mountaineers because ropes and ice axes are required.

Noble Creek is 200 m past this side trail, and one kilometre past this creek there is an interesting side trip to see the "Twin Falls" and canyon. Small cairns on the right mark an easy bushwhack to this viewpoint.

About 4 km past Noble Creek the trail is forced closer to the river by big cliffs and crosses the Bedwell River again (and for the last time) at Ashwood Creek. [42] This is a very tricky crossing so be extra cautious. Once you are across, a spacious campsite can be found a 5-10 minutes' walk up the trail along a dry creek bed that leads off to the left. This fine gravel bar campsite has an open view of the whole valley and Big Interior Mountain. The average hiker should reach this spot, about 14 km from tidewater, in about 5-8 hours.

Map C5

Once you are on the south side of the Bedwell River, after the crossing near Ashwood Creek, you reach an old logging/mining road. Go no more than 45 m or so before swinging to the left. Otherwise you go in the wrong direction, well away from the river. The correct trail does cut away from the river for 1.5 km and then bypasses a 100 m washed-out section before rejoining the main route again. Another kilometre brings you to **You**[i] **Creek**[43] and another potentially dangerous water crossing. An old bridge that once stood here is now completely gone so you must ford the creek.

The old road continues for another 2 km up the valley, as it swings north and begins to climb more steeply. At the end of the old logging road the trail follows a dry creek bed for a short section before turning off to the right (look for flagging tape) to reach the old-growth forest. It is a bit of a test to locate the route in this area, up into the old-growth and through the slide areas. A recently scoured slide near the upper part of the valley makes this section extremely difficult.

A series of old game trails, climbing steeply in sections, brings you into the slide areas by way of a small river crossing. Cairns mark the route across, climbing a bit to again reach the old-growth trees. The trail winds through forest and swampy areas.

Shortly before K2 Creek a small side trail leads to an impressive waterfall, unofficially named "Doran Falls" after two brothers, Stan and George Doran, who rebuilt this section of trail when well into their 70s. A rustic bridge atop a waterfall leads over K2 Creek. The route climbs to the side trail going to Oinimitis Lake and in half an hour, through fragile alpine

---

i   **You Creek:** Named by Norm Stewart after the You Mineral Claim

meadows, you reach Bedwell Lake. The BC Parks trail out to **Thelwood Creek**[i] starts at the campsite at the southeast corner of the lake.[16]

Linked by BC Parks' Bedwell Lake Trail that runs from Thelwood Creek to Bedwell Lake, a through trip from Bedwell Sound to Bedwell Lake will take two to three days (16-20 hours), with a further day (2-4 hours) to reach the Jim Mitchell Lake road. Further hiking options are available at Bedwell Lake. You can follow a rugged route to the Price Creek Trail via Cream Lake (14 km of difficult terrain taking one to two days and not recommended as a through route by BC Parks. See route (c) in Section 2, page 72.) Your second choice is to go out on an equally challenging route via the Drinkwater Creek Valley, Della Falls and Great Central Lake (boat or canoe needed).

Buttle Lake Trails

Buttle Lake was named after John Buttle, a member of the Vancouver Island Exploration Expedition of 1864, and leader of a group who, in 1865, discovered this long (32 km) narrow lake running north-south in the interior of Vancouver Island. The lake provides very important marine and road access into the central area of Strathcona Park. The paved Buttle Lake (Parkway) Road, which follows the east shore, leaves Highway 28 (the Gold River highway) at the Buttle Narrows bridge (47.7 km west of the junction of Highways 19, 19A and 28, near Campbell River) and runs south to end at the Boliden Mine. As you drive a few kilometres south of the narrows, glance west over Buttle Lake, a little below where the Wolf River enters the lake, for a glimpse of **Mount Haig-Brown (1948 m)** named after Campbell River's well-known writer, Roderick Haig-Brown, and his wife, Anne. The summit is directly north of **Mount Con Reid**[ii] **(1744 m)**. **Backcountry camping fees apply at various Buttle Lake marine campsites and one on Upper Campbell Lake.**

(a) Lupin Falls Nature Walk (not shown on our maps)

About 8 km south of the Buttle Narrows bridge find this trail signposted by BC Parks. A 20-minute loop nature walk through an open "big tree" forest brings you to Lupin Falls[iii]. At lakeside there are some picnic tables and walking access to the beach.

---

i **Thelwood Creek:** Ethel Wood was wife of G. Cory Wood, MLA for Alberni, 1912-14.

ii **Mount Con Reid:** Norm Stewart named the mountain in 1936 after a resident guide and hunter.

iii **Lupin Falls:** This is a misspelling of the name of the wild lupines that flower here.

(b) Jack's Augerpoint Trail (Map C3)

The start is located off the Buttle Lake (Parkway) Road about 20.5 km south of the Highway 28 junction at the Buttle Narrows bridge (or 2.4 km if going north from Karst Creek boat ramp.) Look for roadside parking. The old **Augerpoint Trail**[i] was burned out in a forest fire and is still unusable, but Jack Shark (a member of CDMC) constructed a trail that goes up north of the burn. The start of this unofficial trail is 550 m north of the old trail and is flagged, but not signposted except for a red line on the highway. It is narrow and steep at times and there are several hazardous spots. In about two hours you reach a little pond where you can camp, and three hours beyond the pond, at the 1400 m level, the trail breaks out into the sub-alpine of a pleasant plateau with small ponds and good camping opportunities. The trail turns south for a half mile to link up with the old trail, and this section has now been slashed out and marked. **Note: This route is not endorsed nor maintained by BC Parks.**

If travelling west from Ruth Masters Lake, do not go down the old trail to Buttle Lake, which seems nice at the start but will drop you into the burned area. Continue north for one kilometre to an area of small ponds (good camping) and descend from there on a steep trail. See also the Augerpoint route, Section 2 (h), page 82.

(c) Augerpoint Fire Trail (Map C3)

This trail, suitable for all ages, is a 15 - 20 minute walk through an area burned during the Augerpoint fire. The trail starts from the picnic area, just over a kilometre south of Jack's Augerpoint Trail.

(d) Karst Creek Trail (Map C3)

The trail, around 23 km south of the Buttle Narrows bridge, is suitable for all ages and is signposted at the Karst Creek day-use area. Here there is swimming, picnicking and a boat launch. The latter used to be called the Ralph River Boat Ramp. The creek disappears into limestone[ii] and the 45 minute loop trail returns along the beautiful valley floor.

(e) Shepherd Creek Loop Trail (Map C3)

The trailhead is directly across Buttle Lake (Parkway) Road from the BC Parks Ralph River campground, about 26 km south of the Buttle Narrows bridge. This interesting one-kilometre nature walk features a Pacific

---

i **Augerpoint Mountain:** William Ralph, an early surveyor, named the peak in 1936 for its shape.

ii See footnote, page 186.

dogwood tree and a marshy area. For its first 200 m the trail follows the bank of the creek, and it has an overall elevation gain of 50 m.

(f) Shepherd Creek Rescue Route (Maps C4 and C3)

Hikers on the high ridges east of Buttle Lake have few routes to follow when escaping bad weather. This rescue trail was worked on by hiking club volunteers in order to provide some help to those trying to drop down to Buttle Lake and the highway, near the Shepherd Creek[i] Loop Trail. A thick growth of small hemlocks impedes some lower stretches of the route.

(g) Lower Myra Falls Trail (Map C4)

One kilometre beyond Thelwood Creek bridge at the south end of Buttle Lake (and 1 km from the end of the paved road) turn onto a gravel road leading to a signed parking area, and follow a gentle walking trail down to Myra Falls. This one-kilometre walk takes 20-40 minutes and features old-growth forest and a good view of these impressive multiple falls.

(h) Marble Meadows Trail (Map C3)

From the Buttle Narrows bridge drive south about 23 km to the Karst Creek boat ramp if using a boat, or to the Augerpoint picnic area (to the north) if using a canoe. When landing at BC Parks' Marine Site at Phillips Creek watch for underwater stumps. The trail starts on the north side of the creek and is well graded to a creek and camping spot halfway.

The trail then becomes steeper up to alpine meadows. This trail was constructed as a Centennial project by IMR and CDMC with the help of BC Parks. Time up to the Wheaton Hut area is about 5 hours (some groups with heavy packs require 7 hours). This hut is very small but was clean and in decent repair in 2001. The biffy is gone, though. Hikers should depend on using tents. See also Section 2, route (f), page 79.

(i) Flower Ridge Trail (Maps C4 and C5)

This trail is steep, rough, and there is a lack of water. It is not recommended for novices. The trailhead is about 3.5 km south of Ralph River campsite (signposted by **Henshaw Creek**[ii]). Elevation gain up to the ridge is about 1160 m, over about 6 km. Time up, 4 or 5 hours; down, 2½ to 3 hours. The first part of the trail is well-defined through beautiful, open woods. Although steep in places because the trail lacks switchbacks, there are

---

i   **Shepherd Creek**: F.H. Shepherd surveyed the E&N Railway in 1909.
ii **Henshaw Creek:** The name appears on a 1913 map; Henshaw may have been a prospector.

some level and downhill sections. After the first hour there are two or three side trails which lead to viewpoints overlooking Buttle Lake and the mountains. Further up, a burn area affords good views of Mount Myra. This can make a good day hike. To reach the alpine area at the top of the ridge where you get the best views, and there are some nice ponds to camp by, you should allow plenty of daylight hours. See also Section 2, routes (b), page 70, and (c), page 72.

(j) Price Creek Trail (Maps C4 and C5)

BC Parks does not recommend the use of this access to Cream Lake[i]. The preferred route is via the Bedwell Lake Trail. (See (l), page 55.) Due to major impacts of camping in this area, there is a camping fee for the entire corridor from Price Creek[ii] to Cream Lake and out to the Bedwell Lake trailhead. Random camping is permitted along Price Creek and is discouraged at Cream Lake. Campers here are subject to the camping fees even though facilities are not provided. Please camp at the developed sites to minimize impact to the area. Camping fees are $5 per person (16 years and older), per night (2002). No fires are permitted.

The Price Creek Trail (see photo page 95) is located at the head of Buttle Lake, approximately 34.5 km south of the Buttle Narrows bridge and Highway 28 junction (or 8.5 km south of the Ralph River campsite). The trail is recommended for strong hikers and gains 1200 m of elevation over 8.5 km and takes about seven hours one way. Members of the CDMC have relocated the upper part of this old elk trail, which provides difficult access to Cream Lake. The route, which receives little maintenance other than sporadic clearing, stays on the east side of Price Creek right up to the Cream Lake Junction [13]. Here a log crosses Price Creek (with hand cable). This arduous route parallels the north side of Cream Creek to about 275 m below Cream Lake, then crosses an open slide area up above the east side of the creek. The worst of the slide areas are skirted but the upper part is a very steep chute. The route is physically challenging, especially with a heavy pack, but not particularly technical. Ropes may be needed along the steep sections.

The trail is obvious for the first bit, but at the base of an avalanche chute, the markers disappear. Unfortunately, unless you know exactly where the chute is, route finding can be a dilemma since the avalanche zone can't be

---

i   **Cream Lake** gets its name from its opaque, milky appearance.

ii   **Price Creek** is named after the Hon. Price Ellison, who led a 1910 expedition up the Campbell River into what is now Strathcona Park. Ellison was instrumental in the creation of the park in 1911.

seen through the trees. Some forking in Cream Creek and a lot of blowdown in the forest roughly marks the elevation of the chute. Turn east to cross the creek and ascend the avalanche chute (in spring and summer, of course) and head to a small snowfield above it and to the left. It's a short hike from the snowfield to Cream Lake [14]. The route skirts Cream Lake's north side, crosses the outlet stream and parallels the west shore. See also Section 2, routes (c), page 72, and (i), page 83.

(k) Thelwood Lake Route (Maps C4 and C5)

At the head of Buttle Lake, drive on Boliden roads to the parking lot at the start of the Bedwell Lake Trail. Access from here to Jim Mitchell Lake[i] (flooded 1985) is made either on foot or by four-wheel-drive vehicle only. A small parking lot is provided just before Jim Mitchell Lake. The old connecting road to the Price Creek access road (which appears on the federal NTS map) is washed out and will not be restored. Camping is not permitted at or near the dam. These roads will not be ploughed in winter.

There is no easy access from Jim Mitchell Lake dam to the Thelwood Lake area. It is advisable to take a canoe to the head of Jim Mitchell Lake then hike a rough bush route, made by Westmin (now Boliden) employees, that follows the south side of the creek to Thelwood Lake.

(l) Bedwell Lake Trail (Maps C4 and C5)

Due to a concern that the Bedwell Lake area's natural resources could become depleted, BC Parks has designated the Bedwell Lake corridor as a core area within which campfires are banned. Camp stoves are required. To lessen impact to the area, camping is allowed only at the developed campsites at Bedwell and Baby Bedwell[ii] lakes. Camping fees are $5 per person (16 years and older), per night (2002). BC Parks recommends the Bedwell Lake Trail for those hiking to Cream Lake.

BC Parks has developed the Bedwell Lake Trail as an opportunity for less-experienced hikers to access an alpine/subalpine area, especially on a day-use basis. This trail links with the Bedwell River Trail to form a through route between the Pacific Ocean (at Bedwell Sound) and Buttle Lake.

black bear tracks

---

i   According to Karl Stevenson in his *Hiking in Strathcona Park* (1974), in 1937 "a party of surveyors were camped near Thelwood Lake, and they sent **Jim Mitchell** out for supplies. When he didn't come back, they went looking for him, and found his body some distance downstream from a log which was used to cross Thelwood Creek." Jim was only seventeen.

ii   **Baby Bedwell Lake:** This is the unofficial name for the lake immediately north of Bedwell Lake.

There are many black bears in this area, and a management concept is being developed to prevent bear habitat from being disturbed by visitors. You will help by only camping in the designated areas at Bedwell and Baby Bedwell lakes. Perhaps this background will help you, as you walk this trail, to think about the difficulties of managing recreation use in wilderness areas.

The use of steel stairways on this trail continues to offend some hikers while being appreciated by others. This trail is now extremely popular and a significant impact on a sensitive and fragile area is the result. Visitors to the area can protect the wilderness qualities of this beautiful area by practising low impact techniques. One of the best ways to see this area without further impacting it is to visit as a day hiker. With just a daypack, you'll find that the trail will flow beneath your feet and you will gain elevation without stress.

To **access** the trailhead from the south end of Buttle Lake, leave the Buttle Lake (Parkway) Road (35 km from the Buttle Narrows bridge and Highway 28 junction) and head for Jim Mitchell Lake (Map C4). Follow the signs about 6.8 km up a rough two-wheel-drive road to the trailhead information shelter and parking area.

The trail is 6 km long, gains 600 m in elevation, and takes about three hours. It ascends a steep forested valley with numerous bridge crossings and then breaks out into a hilly subalpine area with two lakes and many tarns and creeks. As shown on Map C5, there is designated camping at Baby Bedwell Lake, with six tent platforms and a pit toilet, and on the east shore of Bedwell Lake[16], where there are ten tent platforms and a toilet.

Note: It will be obvious to experienced campers that this kind of environment is very susceptible to the impacts of human use. At this altitude plants have a very short growing season and cannot recover from trampling. Soil cover in the alpine is thin and easily washed away if it is disturbed, for example, by trenching around tent sites. Restrict your hiking to marked trails. Use the toilets, not the bushes, and wash well away from the lake so your wash water filters through the ground.

The route between Bedwell and Cream lakes is described in Section 2, end of part (c), page 72. It takes one to three hours, one way. Other side trips from Bedwell Lake include hikes up **Mount Tom Taylor[i]** and **Big Interior Mountain (1862 m)**, each requiring a full day. See Section 2, route (d), page 74, for the route from Bedwell Lake to Burman Lake. The Oinimitis Trail down to the Bedwell River also begins at [16]. See page 48.

---

i   The Hon. **Thomas Taylor** was Minister of [Public] Works, 1908-1915.

Boliden (formerly Westmin) Mine Area

The Boliden mine site is about 40 km south of the Buttle Narrows bridge (or 13.5 km south of the Ralph River campground). Where Highway 28 swings west to cross the bridge at the narrows, keep straight ahead (south) on Buttle Lake (Parkway) Road. At the head of Buttle Lake continue beyond the mine to the visitors' parking lot. Cars may be left here for the duration of the hike, but no camping is permitted in or around the parking lot. Until 4:00 pm, Boliden may be reached at (250) 287-9271. Hikers may use the recreation building pay phone to arrange to be picked up. In the case of an emergency, the company office will help contact authorities to arrange helicopter evacuation.

(a) Phillips Ridge Trail   (MAP C4)

This well-constructed trail affords access to the high ridge tour of the Phillips Ridge watershed without the need to cross Buttle Lake by boat. Drive through the mine site to the parking area, then walk about 30 m past the yellow gate on the gravel road and turn right at the BC Parks sign. The trail starts at the 360 m level and switchbacks up to the 1300 m level. It passes through open woods up to Arnica Lake and then enters alpine meadows and ridges.

Hikers are now directed around the east side of the lake only, and the old camp and trails are now a reclamation area. Fire pits have been eradicated. Five tent platforms have been installed at a dedicated campsite and a boardwalk provides lakeshore access. BC Parks has installed a pit toilet and a bear-proof cache at the northeast side of the lake, not far from the campsite. In order to help protect this area from unintentional abuse, BC Parks has erected an educational sign describing ethics for backcountry users.

Hiking time to **Arnica Lake**[i], 3 to 4 hours; with large packs, four to five hours. First available water is at 460 m, a few minutes past the waterfalls; second water at 730 m; next at Arnica Lake, 1300 m. Areas around the lake and the shoulders of Mount Phillips have beautiful seasonal flowers. This is a fairly strenuous day hike. See also Section 2, route (f), page 79.

This trail was initiated by Don Apps of the Comox District Mountaineering Club (CDMC) and has been a joint project of BC Parks and the Federation of Mountain Clubs of BC. Upgrades are done mainly by CDMC and Island Mountain Ramblers (IMR) volunteers.

---

i   Mountain **Arnica** (*Arnica latifolia*), with its bright yellow daisy-like flowers, is found at higher elevations.

(b) Upper Myra Falls Trail (Maps C4 and B4)

Having parked as above, walk past the gate on the gravel road about 800 m to where the trail cuts into the bank on the right side. Follow the markers (placed by CDMC). This is a nice valley walk on a fair trail through mature trees. There is one creek crossing on a new bridge. At the end of the trail by the falls, BC Parks has built a lookout platform. Time - one hour each way.

As part of the Adopt-A-Trail program organized by the Federation of Mountain Clubs of BC, this trail and its maintenance was formally adopted in 1991 by the CDMC. This was the first Adopt-A-Trail project on Vancouver Island.

(c) Mount Thelwood Route from Myra Creek
(Maps C4 and B4)

As above, follow the Upper Myra Falls Trail for about half an hour. Just past an area of blowdown the trail turns southwards, downhill, to a fork in the creek. The creek crossing can be difficult during the spring when water levels are high. From here the route is sparsely flagged to the centre of the ridge, and then follows the ridge as a bushwhack. This flagged (once upon a time) route (marked by CDMC) gives easy and short access to the Thelwood area. During summer there can be a serious problem finding water. The ridge itself is dry, and it is a long way from Myra Creek to alpine areas where water may be found. Be sure to carry sufficient amounts of water. See also the relevant paragraph of route (d), on page 74.

(d) Boliden to Tennent Lake to Mount Myra
(Map C4)

From the powerhouse above the minesite follow the penstock road up to Tennent Lake (very rough and steep). Turn south near the lakeshore and look for flagging tape markers. The route (rough, with many windfalls) leads around to the east side of the ridge and terminates at a rock slope (not too steep). Above is a semi-alpine area on the northwest ridge, which you follow up to the summit. Two alternate routes to the top of **Mount Myra**[i] **(1808 m)** start along the old road near East Tennent Creek. Myra's northwest ridge is excellent, even in winter, when trees provide anchorage for the slopes leading up the ridge.

---

i **Mount Myra** and **Myra Lake, Creek and Falls**, may have been named by Price Ellison after his daughter, Myra, who accompanied him on an exploratory trip in 1910, or by Mike King (who explored Buttle Lake by canoe prior to 1900) after Myra Cliffe, daughter of Samuel Cliffe, a Comox pioneer. Visit the BC Geographical Names website (see page 30) to join the debate.

Trails From Highway 28 (Gold River Highway)

(a) Lady Falls Trail (not shown on our maps)

On Highway 28, drive 16.7 km west of the Buttle Narrows bridge. Watch for the parking area, on the left side of the highway. A short but steep trail climbs up to Lady Falls, a clamorous cascade on **Cervus Creek**[i]. Stay well back from the cliff.

(b) Kings Peak Access Route (Map A1)

On Highway 28, drive approximately 19.5 km west from the Buttle Narrows bridge and turn left on the Elk River Timber (ERT) logging road (just after the highway passes under a power transmission line). One kilometre later, park at a pulloff on the left before the logging road crosses the Elk River. Just beyond the power line clearing, the trail climbs to a small creek crossing and joins the access route on the other side. An alternative is to drive the power line dirt road (the gate may be locked) and link up with the standard route as shown on the map.

This trail is steep in sections and most groups with full pack will take 5 to 6 hours to reach the upper bowl. In the spring, caution is required where the trail opens into a curved gully just below the north bowl. Avalanches can funnel into the gully, from which hikers have no fast exit. After reaching the snow bowl, near the campsite in the meadow, it's safer to take the West Ridge Summer Route rather than continuing south on the gully route. During the summer or even late spring, the latter is dangerous and prone to avalanches.

The summer route crosses the north bowl in a southwest direction. Go up a small hill and through a band of trees (remnant flags) to access a large hanging valley directly north of the feature known locally, but not officially, as "The Queen" of "The Queen's Ridge". From here cross the drainage and climb a distinct route to the valley's southwest corner. Ascend an obvious, long, straight gully to the top of the ridge. A good "bivvy boulder" (place to bivouac, or shelter, during bad weather or emergency) sits beside the trail on the flat bench about halfway between the crest of the gully and "The Queen". The route winds around the back (southwest) side of the ridge, then goes almost directly over the summit of "The Queen", drops

---

i   **Cervus** is Latin for "deer", and the local elk are *Cervus canadensis*.

---

into the col[i] between "The Queen" and Kings Peak, then up to the top of **Kings Peak**[ii] **(2065 m)**.

In the winter, avalanches threaten the gully and lower approaches. The West Ridge Winter Route begins farther down the valley, enters a short gully and continues up to the ridge. There are no ribbons and the start is hard to find. This route has been adopted by **The Heathens Mountaineering Club**[iii] .

(c) Elk River Trail (Maps A1 and A2)

BC Parks has established a fee collection zone and a no-camping area for the Elk River corridor. Use only the designated campsites at Butterwort Creek and the Upper Gravel Bar, below Landslide Lake. Camping is not allowed at Landslide Lake or at the glacial lake at the foot of Mount Colonel Foster. The camping fee in the Elk River Trail corridor is $5 a person (16 years and older), per night (2002).

At the Buttle Narrows bridge, (47.7 km west of the junction of Highways 19, 19A and 28, near Campbell River) stay on Highway 28, and continue another 23.7 km west toward Gold River. Watch for signs to the trailhead. Driving time from Campbell River is about 1 hour. The trailhead is 16 km east of Gold River.

The trail is essentially an old elk trail that has been improved over the years, first by a government crew, then by some members of the Island Mountain Ramblers (IMR), the CDMC, and by BC Parks. The trail is seasonally cleared nicely up to the gravel bar below Landslide Lake and upper river flats. It is now quite a good trail and the hazardous log crossings at **Butterwort**[iv], **Volcano**[v] and **Puzzle**[vi] creeks have been replaced by sturdy

---

i a **col**, or **saddle**, is a depression in a ridge or mountain chain.

ii **Kings Peak:** Michael and James King were members of the Ellison expedition in 1910.

iii The name of this club refers to those who prefer **"the heath"**, or the high areas where the heather grows, and not necessarily to the philosophical beliefs of the members.

iv Common **butterwort** (*Pinguicula vulgaris*) grows along the banks of the creek. It's an insect-eating plant with single purple flowers borne on stems above fleshy leaves. According to Pojar and MacKinnon's *Plants of Coastal British Columbia* (BC Ministry of Forests and Lone Pine Publishing, 1994), butterwort was considered by Yorkshire farm women to have a positive effect on the productivity of milk cows, thus ensuring the butter supply. It was even thought to "protect cows from elf arrows and humans from witches and fairies."

v **Volcano Lake** is a lake within a cirque, resembling a volcanic crater.

vi **Puzzle Mountain** is named for its maze of snow drifts.

bridges built by the IMR in conjunction with BC Parks. At Volcano Creek there have been numerous bear sightings.

Due to the popularity of this trail, BC Parks has developed management strategies to protect the area from the effects of human use, and abuse. This includes concentrating tent camping at sites that can take the impact. The Butterwort Creek and Upper Gravel Bar locations are shown on Maps A1 and A2. It is about a three-hour hike for a hiker with full overnight gear to the Butterwort Creek gravel bar, and about six hours to the Gravel Bar Campsite. From here you can make day excursions, especially to Landslide Lake. **Camping is not allowed at Landslide Lake or at the glacial lake at the foot of Mount Colonel Foster**. See also Section 2, routes (e), page 78, and (j), page 83.

During the strong earthquake of June 24, 1946, a part of **Mount Colonel Foster[i] (2135 m)** fell away into Landslide Lake below. The water was displaced so violently that it caused havoc in this part of the valley, taking out hundreds of trees, down to bedrock, for about 800 m. This scar is still clearly visible.

To Landslide Lake.

Though part of a main route to the Golden Hinde (three to four days one way) the Elk River Trail is used mostly by those who want to hike in to Landslide Lake. They camp en route and take a daypack on the second day, either camping a second night or heading out.

At about 9.5 km a side trail to Landslide Lake leaves the Elk River Trail (map A2) after it crosses the outfall stream, near the BC Parks bridge. A trail climbs to the side of a waterfall (very impressive in flood) and leads to Landslide Lake. **Camping at Landslide Lake is not permitted.** For those en route to the Golden Hinde this makes a pleasant lunch break provided backpacks are stashed and not carried up to the lake and then down again.

(d) Crest Mountain Trail   (Map A1)

From the Buttle Narrows bridge, stay on Highway 28 and drive just under 25 km to the Drum Lake Narrows. Watch for the signposted parking area. Cross the Narrows by bridge onto a clearly defined trail that is graded at the lower levels. The trail was originally constructed by the BC Forest Service

---

i   **Colonel (later Major-General) William W. Foster** (1875-1954), served as Deputy Minister of Public Works, as a distinguished soldier in W.W. I, as president of a major company, as Chief of Police for Vancouver, and as a special commander for defence projects in W.W. II, but it was as "Billy Foster" that he, along with A.H. MacCarthy, made the first undisputed ascent of Mount Robson. He also served as president of the ACC, 1922-1924.

for a study of climatic conditions. No longer used for this purpose, the trail has deteriorated higher up. At the 550 m level a tree has been felled to cross the creek, but it is not always needed. Beyond this level the trail becomes steep, but even those who do not go up the whole way will find there are some fine viewpoints.

Time up to 1440 m level and an alpine lake is about four hours. Budget your time to continue another kilometre to the rounded top and to explore the ridge northwards. This alpine area is a continuation of the alpine mountain ridges, but is not part of the interconnecting route system previously described. On good days there are spectacular views in all directions, especially south across the valley towards Kings Peak, **Elkhorn Mountain**[i] and Mount Colonel Foster.

Crest Creek Crags, 2.5 km west of the Crest Mountain Trail, has become a very well known rock climbing area. However, non-designated camping within one kilometre of a highway is not allowed in BC's provincial parks, so you are advised not to camp here. BC Parks closely monitors this area.

Donner Lake Access

Donner Lake[ii] is a popular fishing destination, and a canoe/hiking access route into Strathcona Park mountains. The lake is accessed by old logging roads, which are in poor condition, sometimes washed out and impassable by vehicle. The area reached by the road seems to be used by the four-wheel-drive party crowd, and you should be cautious about leaving your vehicle, or camping overnight. Locked gates may restrict access.

In the town of Gold River, heading west, take the second left turn after the arena entrance, onto a paved road (Ucona Main) signed "To the Re-cycling Plant". Stay on this road (now dirt) for 12 km to Star Lake. Three kilometres past the lake, take the first left turn (U7). From here on, a high-slung four-wheel-drive vehicle is needed. Next turn right onto the Western Forest Products (WFP) road to Kunlin Lake, and drive around the lake to Donner Falls. Park here and walk up beside the river to Donner Lake. Reports in 2002 indicated trees had been felled along the road beyond Kunlin Lake, precluding vehicular entry.

---

i   According to Karl Stevenson in his *Hiking in Strathcona Park* (1974), when members of ACC made the first ascent of the mountain in 1912, it was known as "the Matterhorn of Strathcona Park." Since it was close to the Elk River, they suggested calling it **"Elkhorn"**.

ii   According to Allan C. Brooks, Julius and Charles **Donner** had a cabin on this lake 1907-1911.

Gold Lake Access (Map A0)

There are two routes into **Gold Lake**[i]. Due to limited trail clearing and maintenance both accesses are overgrown and hard to locate. All streams flood and some are impassable when rain is heavy. Snowfall in this area is abundant and the snowpack holds into late June. Expect rougher roads closer to Gold Lake (a high-slung four-wheel-drive may be required). Seasonal washouts and snows may block area roads.

From the east :

From the junction of Highway 19, Highway 19A and Highway 28 in Campbell River, stay north on Highway 19 for about 14.5 km to Weyerhaeuser's Menzies (Salmon River) Main. Check on access and road conditions with Weyerhaeuser's North Island Timberlands if your hike is planned early in the year. Use Weyerhaeuser's *Recreation and Logging Road Guide to TFL 39*. (See *Logging Companies* on page 24.)

All roads are open except those in active logging areas. Access may not be possible in dry weather due to the extreme fire hazard. Observe all signs.

Turn left (west) onto Menzies (Salmon River) Main, past a company work yard and drive 15.2 km to Brewster Lake's south end. Cross the bridge and continue west another 30 km (via the Salmon River and Grilse Creek valleys) to the start of the trail (signposted) at Spur H. There is limited parking here. Only four-wheel-drive vehicles can proceed (and not very far) along the nearby spur road.

From the west:

Western Forest Products has opened access to the west side of Gold Lake with the construction of a logging road (the upper stretches may require a four-wheel-drive vehicle with good clearance) which passes through the northwest corner of Strathcona Provincial Park to access timber outside the park boundary. Use WFP's *Visitors Guide to Logging Roads and Recreation Areas (Nootka Region)*.

Drive 3 km north from Gold River and cross the lofty Gold River bridge to a signposted T-junction. Swing right onto Nimpkish Road heading toward Woss. (A left goes to the Upana Caves and Tahsis.) About 6.5 km north from the Gold River bridge, cut right (east) onto East Main to begin the climb up the Gold River Valley. Keep right at the Y junction. The road cuts through **Gold / Muchalat Provincial Park (653 ha)**. Visited mainly by anglers, the region has stands of old-growth trees and is home to deer and Roosevelt elk.

---

i   **Gold Lake** is named for ore found in the area.

East Main has a strange one-way section that could be dangerous if you miss it and go the wrong way. A little before the Saunders Main junction you'll cross Saunders Creek. At the junction, stay on East Main and travel approximately 2 km to the trailhead. The parking area is on the left side of the road, and the trail is difficult to find and overgrown with bush. The route is in poor condition but the distance to Gold Lake is only 2 to 3 km.

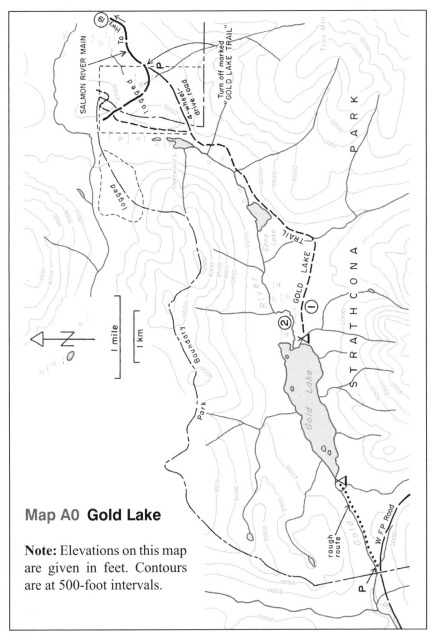

Map A0 Gold Lake

Note: Elevations on this map are given in feet. Contours are at 500-foot intervals.

Section 2

The Backcountry Routes of Strathcona Park

NOTE: The term "backcountry" refers to the park's more remote areas, with wilderness camping and no amenities.

*The following sub-sections describe in some detail a selection of backcountry routes in Strathcona Park. It is assumed that those travelling these routes are experienced hikers or climbers, competent at map reading and route finding, and equipped with map, compass and altimeter. Many hikers also use a GPS. It is important that you read "**Hiking in Strathcona Park**", page 28; "**How To Use This Book**", page 14; and "**Hints and Cautions**", page 15, before reading further.*

Off-road horse riding and bicycling are not allowed anywhere in the park and a penalty fine is in place for violations. BC Parks discourages the marking of routes by any means. Painting or other the use of other permanent markers is illegal.As of 2003, new regulations will prohibit campfires anywhere in the backcountry of Strathcona Provincial Park.

Once again we state that it is with some misgiving that we publish these details, as the alpine and sub-alpine areas, through which these routes go, are easily damaged irreparably by over-use and, above all, by thoughtless camping practices. With society's growing awareness of a need to preserve some of the outdoors in its natural state, it is to be hoped that considerate visitors will use Strathcona Park without ruining the very landscape they came to enjoy.

A special feature of Strathcona Park is the way high alpine ridges interconnect, enabling long traverses and circular tours of the park to be made mostly above tree line. This section of the book takes the form of a route description for an extended backpacking trip that, by following the system of interconnecting ridges, takes us right through Strathcona Park from east to south and then west to north. In reality, such a trip is possible and would take about three weeks, though re-supplies of food would be a logistical challenge.

Starting from Mount Becher in the Forbidden Plateau section of the Park, the ridges are followed southwards to Comox Glacier, then west to Mount Septimus and Big Interior Mountain, north to Mount Thelwood, thence following the height of land to Burman Lake, passing south of the Golden Hinde and continuing in a northwesterly direction on the height of land and down to the Elk River valley. This route is almost entirely in alpine parkland or high alpine, only dropping into the timber for two short sections through its entire length.

Most hikers will hike this route a section at a time, so the text is divided into sections, which can be used as needed. The maps in this book show the access points to this high-level route; for trail descriptions see Section 1.

In addition, this part of the book describes other high-level routes that can be enjoyed individually or in combination, including a number of loop routes that return you to where (or almost where) you started. For example, four such trips, each of about a week's duration, may be made from Buttle Lake.

Probably the most popular, and the easiest, circular tour is that which starts and ends at Phillips Creek, traversing the entire Phillips Creek watershed boundary by way of the high divide, including Marble Meadows[i] in the route. It is, of course, necessary to cross the lake by boat to reach Phillips Creek.[ii]

Another tour follows the trail from Buttle Lake to Augerpoint, and circles the Ralph River watershed, arriving back at Ralph River campground, about 5 km south of the starting point. Then, starting from Ralph River campsite, you can follow ridges around the Shepherd Creek watershed and back to starting point. The last and shortest of this quartet, also starting from Ralph River, circles the Henshaw Creek watershed and includes the Flower Ridge Trail.

A weather caution. Those who travel in high areas should always keep a careful watch for changes in the weather. Check long-range weather predictions prior to your hike. Even in summer a major storm lasting for two or three days can occur, and it can be quite cold, with high winds in exposed areas. A big storm usually takes at least half a day to get started, so those who get caught unawares have generally themselves to blame. If one seems to be blowing up, stop at a good campsite, even as early in the day as noon, for in such circumstances it is better to camp early than to press on until late in the day, when, cold, wet and tired, you may have to settle for an indifferent spot.

For weather information visit: www.weatheroffice.ec.gc.ca.

---

i   **Marble Meadows:**The name comes from the limestone (marble) formations.

ii **Note:** It is possible to make the same tour starting and ending at Boliden minesite, using the Phillips Ridge access trail and thus avoiding the need for a boat. It means, however, that you have to hike up to alpine not once, but twice, each time a six-hour climb with a full pack.

When seeking a campsite for bad weather it may be best to drop down from the alpine terrain 300 m or so into the timber, preferably on south- or west-facing slopes, where Douglas-fir is found at higher elevation than it is on slopes facing north and east. Here one may camp with good shelter. When the weather improves, an hour's hike or so will have you back on the ridges and the detour will have been well worthwhile for the extra comfort it provided while the storm raged.

When travelling in the timber, full use should be made of game trails. Deer and elk trails often are the best routes along valley floors and up the timbered ridges to the alpine zone. Avoid the bottoms of V-shaped valleys and make for the ridges instead. Flat-bottomed valleys often have good game trails beside the creek or on a flat bench 30 m or so above it.

When choosing a route for approaching an unfamiliar mountain, remember that unlogged ridges are generally better going than valleys or draws and that, in central Vancouver Island, south- and west-facing slopes below 1230 m are less bushy than those facing north and east. Above this level the reverse is true. Douglas-fir forest is clearer to walk through than cedar and hemlock. From afar you can tell cedar from fir by its yellow/green hue. Avoid a slope with many dead trees; their bare branches let the light in and make it bushy underfoot.

Going up a mountain, all the ridges converge towards the summit, which is consequently hard to miss. But coming down, it is very easy, in cloud, to pick the wrong ridge, and perhaps come down in the wrong valley. An altimeter is a worthwhile addition to the essential map and compass. On the descent, when the ridge suddenly divides, knowledge of your altitude should enable you to pinpoint your position accurately and pick the right route. If you went up in clear weather and are coming down in cloud, it all looks so different that every landmark you noticed and remembered from the ascent will be appreciated. Remember that if the weather is worsening the barometer is probably falling and the altimeter will probably read high. A change of one kilopascal in barometric pressure represents about 90 m error in altitude (or, a change of ¼" of mercury represents an error of about 250 ft. in altitude). Many hikers now carry a GPS to be used in conjunction with (not as a replacement for) a map and compass.

Read about **safe glacier travel** in *Hints and Cautions* on page 15 and also see page 39, Comox Glacier Trail / Route.

(a) Mount Albert Edward to Comox Glacier

(Maps D2, D3, D4)

This is one tough trip, and it follows rocky barren ridges that provide few sheltered spots able to accommodate more than a couple of tents. However, there is a rugged beauty to the route, especially if you appreciate interesting rocks.

Map D2

This route leaves the main route up Albert Edward at the 1880 m level, where the former turns west. If you have already had a full day you may need to camp at one of the small lakes here[i].

Follow the height of land south, up the north side of **Mount Frink**[ii] (the 1960 m ridge west of Castlecrag), go left around the summit rocks and down the centre of the west ridge. Stick to the southeast side of the buttress (there are fewer bluffs) and **contour**[iii] into the col. Don't turn south too soon or you will run into cliffs. At about the 1600 m level[1] above the steep section east of **Charity Lake**[iv], turn south and follow ledges back to regain the centre of the ridge at about the 1540 m level. Continue down the ridge to a good campsite just below the col between Faith Lake and Charity Lake. (Allow about five hours hiking time from the start).

Map D3

For the route around the north peak of **Mount George V**[v], follow open areas up to about the 1630 m level, then contour west across the mountain's north snowfield. At the steep drop-off on the west ridge[2] turn sharp left and follow up this well-defined ridge to about 1810 m, then contour below the steep section and head south towards the main summit. You can either avoid the summit (and more elevation gain or loss) by turning west and descending a rockslide, then back up to the ridge, or go up and over the summit[3], which is not as hard as it looks.

---

i   **Note:** Though you are technically in an established BC Parks "core area", which doesn't allow random camping, you will not be hassled up here if you are through-travellers respecting the environment. BC Parks used a height of land boundary for the core area, so this location was included by default rather than by design. The core area was created to control camping and campfires in the heavily-used lower-elevation area of the Forbidden Plateau.

ii   **Mount Frink:** The name was requested by a university student among the survey party in 1934, to honour his girlfriend, a Miss Frink.

iii   **"To contour"** means to move across terrain at more or less the same elevation, as though you were following a contour line on a map.

iv   There are three lakes: **Faith, Hope, and Charity**; the greatest of these is Charity.

v   **Mount George V** was named for the King in 1935, the year of his silver jubilee.

Proceeding south from Mount George V, follow the height of land. At the 1600 m level drop off ridge to the right, as a cliff band ahead (not shown on the map) blocks the direct route to the col. A game trail [4], leading to a small slide area to the right of the ridge, is easy to follow. Do not drop down the west side any more than necessary for easy contouring around the cliffs, then get back up to the col. The upper end of **Siokum Creek**[i] valley is one of the few sheltered spots on the route, and has some good camping areas.

The main route south is joined by a route from Ralph River at the point marked [5], and continues on a height of land past **Ink Lake**[ii] and **McQuillan Lake**[iii] and on to **Aureole**[iv] **snowfield**. (Note: The Ralph Ridge is a viable escape route.) Follow a line of rock cairns, positioned where necessary to avoid steep sections. Hike south up the snowfield to a low point between the summits of Rees Ridge[v], then head roughly southeast down the main ridge towards the col between **Milla Lake**[vi] and **Mirren Lake**.[vii]

If you are going west to Flower Ridge by way of Tzela Lake[viii] you now have a choice of routes:

If you are hikers rather than climbers, and want to avoid any exposure and use of a rope handline for security, leave Rees Ridge at the 1780 m level and pick your way down the steep southwest side, then down a small side ridge to a point near the outlet of Milla Lake. Cross Shepherd Creek and contour around, a little below the 1230 m level, using open areas, then hike south up the glacier on the west side of **Mount Harmston**[ix] **(1980 m)**, keeping to the west side of the valley to stay clear of steep snow sections. This small glacier does not normally have any dangerous crevasses, but in the last few years of warm winters the ice has become more exposed. While it has receded a fair bit, the toe of the glacier is on relatively flat ground, and this may explain the stability. Keep to the right side near the top, over

---

i   *Siokum* means "in the sun".

ii **Ink Lake** was named by Sid Williams, for its dark colour.

iii **McQuillan Lake**: RCAF Flight Lieutenant Murray McQuillan was killed in W.W. II.

iv Originally named Aureole Snowfield in 1935, for its halo effect, the feature was officially renamed **Aureole Icefield** in 1980.

v   Mr. **Rees** was an old-time prospector who died at the age of 75 on the Mount Becher Trail during the winter of 1933.

vi *Milla* means "white" in the local native language.

vii Karl Stevenson, in *Hiking in Strathcona Park*, says that **Mirren Lake** is named after Mirren Thomas (later Bell) of Courtenay: "In the 1930s, a party of surveyors met a group of girls on the Comox Glacier. The surveyors asked for all the girls' names and decided that Mirren had the prettiest, and so the lake was named."

viii *Tzela* means "heart" in the local native language. (The lake is heart-shaped.)

ix **Mount Harmston**: William Harmston was an early settler in the Comox Valley; Florence Cliffe was his daughter.

the pass and down to regain the main route at the snout of **Cliffe[i] Glacier** [10]. You have to drop 300 m lower this way.

Map D4

If you are climbers, you may choose to follow down the ridge in a southeast direction from [6]. There are good campsites on the south-facing slope of this ridge. (Some climbers take a direct route from the second campsite, around the south end of Milla Lake to [10]. This avoids a lot of up and down travel over Argus Mountain (1980 m). The steep gully marked on Map D4 is loose rock when devoid of snow.) From the col below Rees Ridge, the escarpment looks very spectacular but the route is quite easy, proving the truth of a well-known climber's advice: "you can't judge a mountain till you rub your nose on it" (the late Rex Gibson).

On leaving the col, keep up the ridge to the small glacier, bearing right to follow the moraine between the snow and the top of cliffs above Moving Glacier (exposed). This brings you to a steep gully across your path that runs from the base of the cliffs above [7]. Cross this near its top, using a rope for steep and exposed sections, contour slightly up and across the slope to the right for about 90 m, then climb straight up at the bottom of the cliff to a steep short gully which runs off to the right across the face. Follow this to its top, then climb up a short pitch and you are on the main ridge with Comox Glacier to your left and **Argus Mountain[ii]** and **The Red Pillar[iii] (2031 m)** to your right.

(b) Comox Glacier to Flower Ridge
(Maps D4, C4 and C5)

Continuing from the point where you gained the main ridge, follow a game trail over the small summit at the head of Moving Glacier (steep snow early in the season) and down to the base of the northeast ridge of Argus Mountain. Leave the ridge at this point and angle down across the snow slope on southeast side of Argus to the base of south cliffs, and contour across the south-facing scree slopes above the lower cliffs, working down near the top of lower cliffs, then up again at about 1720 m. The first part of the route

---

i   **Cliffe Glacier:** According to "Origin of Forbidden Plateau Place Names" from Ruth Masters, Florence Cliffe's son, Lucius Cliffe, was the first white boy born north of Nanaimo.

ii   **Argus Mountain:** In his 1974 booklet, *Hiking in Strathcona Park*, Karl Stevenson comments: "Mr. Ben Hughes, editor of the *Comox Argus*, an early newspaper in the Comox Valley, tried to climb the mountain in 1931." Argus means "watchful guardian", so is particularly apt.

iii   **The Red Pillar:** Ben Hughes of the *Argus* wrote that Geoff Capes and Jack Gregson climbed the mountain in 1931 and left a note in a cairn on the summit, suggesting the name "The Pillar".

around the cliff will be steep, exposed snow before July, but it is usually possible to go between the snow and the rocks at the base of the cliff.

The route down off Argus Mountain onto Cliffe Glacier is easy if you pick the correct gully, near a small chimney [8]. Where this gully opens out above a steep section, contour right, then down to the snow. Be cautious here, because where the glacier has melted back it

The Red Pillar and Argus Mountain

leaves a hard sediment, which looks like sand but provides little purchase. High speed, torn clothes and a skinned rear end are likely results. Wear your crampons.

Continue across the glacier southwest to a small low ridge paralleling the west side of the glacier. From here [9] you have a choice of two routes to Tzela Lake. The first starts down near the base of the steep part of The Red Pillar, and into a small side valley leading down to the meadows on the east side of the lake. This is the best route for going to the lake only. The second route goes down a small ridge alongside the glacier. Keep to the glacier side near the lower end and cross the creek below the snout; if the creek is very high you will have to wade across at the snout. Go into the timber facing the end of the ridge, find a game trail about 15 m above the creek and, staying high, well above the creek [10], contour around till you reach an open area. Follow this around to the open flower slopes that angle down to the northwest, and to the large upper flower meadows on the main valley floor. From these meadows, southwards down to Tzela Lake, there is a good game trail which stays on the east side of the stream and leads to camping areas at the north end of the lake.

For the Shepherd Creek ridge route, continue northwards up the main valley to a pass [38]. See also Section 2, route (g), page 81. The Flower Ridge route goes west, across the meadows at about the 1280 m level and, staying to the left of a small side creek and contouring around on open slopes [11], goes up the ridge to the 1540 m level. This upper route will avoid the bushy sections encountered on the lower route starting at Tzela Lake. From here, follow the watershed ridge between the **Ash River**[i] and Henshaw Creek.

---

i **Ash River:** Dr. John Ash was on the committee for the Vancouver Island Exploration Expedition of 1864.

Map C5

The unnamed peak at the head of Henshaw Creek can be bypassed by contouring at the 1600 m level around its southeast side to a small lake at the head of Henshaw Creek. Then follow the ridge centre right up to Flower Ridge.

(c) Flower Ridge to Cream Lake and Bedwell Lake
(Map C5)

Continue southwards, dropping off Flower Ridge at the 1660 m level, into the narrow col [12] between Price Creek and Margaret Lake. From this col there are only two choices if you are hiking: **south**, around the east side of Mount Rosseau and Misthorn[i] to Love Lake or, eventually, Cream Lake, or **west** to join the main Price Creek Trail near the Cream Lake Junction [13].

Price Creek Valley route for hikers: Continue down the Price Creek Valley taking advantage of clear areas at the lower end of slides as much as possible. This route is very difficult to locate due to recent slides and a thick tangle of vegetation. Join Price Creek trail as soon as possible and follow it up to Cream Lake. This will be hard going in the bushy sections. It may not look very far from Flower Ridge to Cream Lake, but allow a day for it. See (i) on page 83.

The Cream Lake area is very fragile. BC Parks does not promote camping near the lake. Your very best no-impact techniques should be stringently applied, including using a stove (no campfires, please), properly burying your excrement (or packing it out) and carefully flaming your toilet paper.

Alternate route for hikers: Follow the ridge south for a kilometre and contour around to the south side of Mount Rosseau[ii] staying below the remnants of glaciers and snow fields. From here hikers to Della Falls Trail can follow a good route to Love Lake (see (b) on page 48). Cross the ridge just below the summit of **Mount Septimus (1935 m)** and descend a snow slope to the south end of Cream Lake [14].

Experienced mountaineers equipped for technical climbing may follow the ridge (not straightforward) south to the summit of **Mount Rosseau (1962 m)** or travel directly to Cream Lake by traversing the north-facing slopes of Septimus and Rosseau. These two routes to Cream Lake are hazardous and are not shown on the maps. They are described below for the benefit of mountaineers only.

---

i   **Misthorn** is now the official name of the peak just east of Mount Rosseau. The name comes from A.O. Wheeler's journal when the Alpine Club of Canada climbed in Strathcona Park in 1912.

ii   **Mount Rosseau:** R.H. Rosseau was a well-known local mountaineer who was killed in 1954 while climbing Mount Arrowsmith.

Upper climbing route: Goes across the top of the glacier above Green Lake, contouring around under a hanging glacier and down to Cream Lake. This route (not shown on our map) is for experienced climbers and only under the best of conditions. For the average hiker there are too many dangers from rock and icefall.

Middle route for experienced climbers: Turn west at the north side of the col and descend to the small green lake on the moraine; follow along the north side of this and cross at the outlet (Price Creek), then contour around under the cliff, taking advantage of open areas and a game trail, until you come to a break in the mountain which forces you down and a little to the right. The rope is needed for a 12 m cliff before you reach an open area at the base of the first large slide coming off Mount Septimus. If you wish to avoid the cliff and don't mind slide alder, continue down alongside Price Creek, and come across to the open area as soon as possible, but don't get down too low.

Climb straight up the big slide, working to the right and keeping out of alder until you get near the base of the cliffs where there is a good game trail; follow this along the cliffs, keeping above the bush in slide areas; cross over the creek coming down from the hanging glacier. Here you will have to go up again, contouring towards Cream Lake as much as possible. The route is not hard to find as there is only one feasible way (glacier above and slides below) and it will put you on the gentle slope above the east side of Cream Lake, with an easy hike down to the lake's south end.

The preferred BC Parks access route to Cream Lake is via the Bedwell Lake Trail. Due to major impacts of camping in this fragile area, there is a camping fee for the entire corridor from Price Creek to Cream Lake and out to the Bedwell Lake trailhead. Random camping is okay along Price Creek but is discouraged at Cream Lake. Campers here are subject to the camping fees even though facilities are not provided. Please camp at the developed sites. Camping fees are $5 per person (16 years and older), per night (2002). Campfires are not permitted within the Bedwell Lake / Price Creek corridor. Carry a portable camp stove.

Continuing on from Cream Lake to Bedwell Lake, follow the trail west around Cream Lake [14] and turn north when you come to a bird's-eye view down Drinkwater Creek of Della Falls. Go west up the small side ridge to the 1350 m level. Follow a bench that continues along this contour (good area for flowers) to the Drinkwater / Bedwell pass [15]. Beyond the pass, on the Bedwell side, go around the north side of the tiny lake (Little Jim Lake) near the watershed. Continue down an open draw to about the 1140 m level, then contour along the side of the ridge and work into the centre as you near the bottom. There is a good game trail with old tapes which is easy to follow and avoids small drops at the centre of the ridge. At the bottom of the ridge area by Bedwell Lake there is a BC Parks campsite with pit toi-lets[16]. (Cream Lake to Bedwell Lake: allow at least one to three hours).

(d) Bedwell Lake to Burman Lake
(Maps C5, B5, B4 and B3)

Allow five days. This section of the route is characterized by glaciated granite, with many hidden drops, which must be circumnavigated. From the camping area [16], go north[i] on the main trail and gain the route around Bedwell Lake by crossing the outfall of Baby Bedwell Lake (see photo page 95). Stay close to the lake shore, and after crossing a stream at the most westerly point of the lake turn west and ascend a moderate slope to about the 1100 m level. From here, the route to the summit of **Mount Tom Taylor (1801 m)** continues continues southwest up a prominent ridge and the cross-country route to Burman Lake turns north, crossing a creek [17] just below its lake outlet and bluff. Ascend the small side ridge north of this lake and head up to the Bedwell / Moyeha pass, then travel northwest following the centre of a ridge for about 800 m.

Map B5

A steep section leads down about 220 m to a very attractive camping area [18] looking across to Taylor Glacier. Continue north by way of a flat open ridge to the lake on the Moyeha River drainage south of Thelwood Lake, bear left at a steep section near the bottom and cross the creek a short way below the outlet. This is the lowest elevation (850 m) on the entire tour. Here, in the western section of the park, north-facing slopes and level areas are open heather due to heavy winter snowfall. South-facing slopes can be bushy (rhododendron) to the 1080 m level.

From the valley floor hike west up the centre of the ridge lying south of Greenview Lake, which is bushy and a little hard to get onto at the lower level, but well-defined and clear going above 950 m. The hump south of Greenview Lake can be contoured around on its southwest side at the 1080 m level, then up into a beautiful, hanging valley with arrow-head-shaped lakes and good camping areas.

---

i   Earlier editions of this book showed routes through the area south of Bedwell Lake. Because there are numerous bears in this region, BC Parks is requesting that hikers stay out of the area, and our route descriptions have been modified accordingly.

Map B4

Continue west past the lakes and swing up to the saddle on the east ridge of **Moyeha Mountain (1794 m)**, and down the other side in a north- westerly direction to about the 1100 m level. At this point [19], you have a choice: around **Mount Thelwood (1731 m)** or over it. For the route around, drop down and cross the creek (open going) then head north up the gully and open slope west of main creek leading to the little "square" lake east of Mount Thelwood. This section makes for very difficult going when there is no snowpack. The east side of the creek does not offer a better alternative. (For a side trip, well worth the effort, go down to the Upper Thelwood Lake and flower meadows.) Pass the "square" lake [20] and go on through the meadows, dropping down to about 1230 m, then contour around on game trail under the cliffs (don't drop too low) to reach heather meadows north of Mount Thelwood.

For the route over Mount Thelwood, contour left from [19] into the pass at base of southwest ridge, then straight up this ridge to the summit. (A route east from here descends to [20] and bypasses the sometimes-difficult route around Mount Thelwood.) From the summit head north across snowfield and so on down to the heather meadows. It is a good route if you have the energy and weather is clear.

From here go north and a little to the east, crossing the low point of an alpine ridge northeast of Thelwood, that divides the north and south branches of Myra Creek[21]. This narrow and well-defined ridge continues eastwards down to the fork. Below 1080 m the ridge is very bushy, but a route has been flagged from here down to the Boliden mine site. See route (c), page 58.

Continuing the main route from[21], drop down 30 m or so, then contour left at about the 1140 m level, up to left of a round hump and a little lake, then north to open slopes leading to the west. Contour around at this level and up to the ridge near the lakes to join the alternate route, described next.

The alternate route to this point, from the heather meadows north of Mount Thelwood, involves more climbing and takes you higher than the above. Hike west from these meadows, and through a pass to an attractive meadow at the head of Bancroft Creek[22]. From the northeast side of this meadow turn north and go up, past a steep area on the right, then east to the 1600 m level. Descend the north ridge and swing right after passing lakes below you on the east side, then generally northwards down a steep section to the outlet of a lake which is part of the Burman River watershed.

Continue north into the timber and contour to the right at 1020 m, then up to the head of larger Harvey Lake from which issues the north fork of Myra

Creek (bushy at low levels). A less bushy route goes east, up the centre of a ridge [23] to a point opposite the west end of Harvey Lake, then down to a heather meadow. This involves about 300 m of climbing, but is well worth it if the bushes are wet. Head north around west end of the lake and climb a 30 m steep section, staying a little to the right. When open alpine is reached, continue north up a gradual slope and past a small lake near the ridge centre, then east along the centre of the ridge to the west peak of Phillips Ridge. Bear right at the steep parts of the lower levels[24]. Halfway up the ridge, the route leaves area of glaciated granite. East of this peak turn north and descend a limestone ridge.

Map B3

After 1½ km, **an alternate route** to **Schjelderup Lake**[i] drops to the west, avoiding the route-finding difficulties and steep, treacherous terrain of the main route, as follows. From the lowest point on Phillips Ridge descend the gully to the west for about 80 m and then traverse to the right at a low angle towards the outlet of **Carter Lake**[ii]. It is a bit scrubby and there is the odd small bluff. There is no distinct trail.

Cross the stream and contour around the southwest side of Carter Lake in open terrain. There is good camping at the lake's north end. Follow the stream up to another small lake under **Mount Burman (1756 m)** and then traverse a small ridge to Schjelderup Lake. Contour around the lake on the west side staying about 40-50 m above the lake for the easiest line to a camping area near [26].

A **second alternate** route swings west at the outlet to Carter Lake and climbs up and over Mount Burman to rejoin the main route to Burman Lake just under a kilometre west of Schjelderup Lake. This second choice passes close to Mount Burman's summit (fine, granite bouldering) and many hikers prefer this traverse. It avoids the thrash down to and around Schjelderup Lake and there is only one big hump to negotiate rather than three. The route is bushy near Carter Lake's south end.) Both alternates avoid a significant elevation gain along Phillips Ridge and, more importantly, some very difficult route-finding between the col, the north end of the ridge, and Schjelderup Lake.

The traditional route follows Phillips Ridge northwards through a region of black rock to a col east of Schjelderup Lake [25]. (The Marble Meadows route

---

i   **Schjelderup Lake:** In 1937, at the age of 16, Roger Schjelderup camped by this lake with Sid Williams and Geoff Capes when they climbed the Golden Hinde. Later, he rose to the rank of Colonel and became the most decorated Canadian officer in W.W. II.

ii **Carter Lake:** Frank Carter was killed in W.W. II.

continues north from this point.) For the Golden Hinde[i] area find a game trail leading steeply down through the meadows and follow it to the end of the meadows and through a thick grove of trees to a very steep grassy clearing with a stream on the right (north). Cross the stream. The route heads to the northwest under the last set of cliffs (at about 1420 m) to gain a side ridge coming up from the lake outlet. The trick is to go below the cliffs (otherwise you bluff out later) but not drop down too far and miss the less difficult section through mature timber on the relatively obscure ridge. Follow down this, just north of centre. As with most east-west ridges between 1080 m and 1540 m in this area, there is clear going just north of ridge centre, due to heavy snow pack. The other side is often bushy.

Some travellers prefer to bypass the somewhat hair-raising drop from the Phillips Ridge to Schjelderup Lake. They start their descent about where the 1600 m mark is shown on Map B3, south of [25]. From this point a long snow gully (partly scree in late summer) descends in a generally westerly direction to the bridge of land between Schjelderup and Carter lakes. Watch for an old CDMC sign on a tree near Schjelderup Lake's southwest corner. Follow the west shore of the lake to [26]. This route depends on the amount of residual snow and lake ice there is, but even in summer there should be only a couple of short, bushy sections. This route is **not** shown on map B3.

From the campsite at Schjelderup Lake's outlet [26] go up the northeast ridge of Mount Burman, where there is clear going on northwest side. (This section west from [26], up the northeast ridge, should be avoided in the winter.) Contour to the west under a steep section to a good ledge leading up and across to join the north ridge below cliffs at 1540 m. Follow this ridge down for about 100 m, then turn west down to meadows above the south bay of Burman Lake. An easy way down may be hard to find, as this is in a zone of glaciated granite.

If backpacking to **Golden Hinde (2200 m)**, continue north down the ridge (if you are bushbashing, and dangling down steep bits holding on to saplings like a trout on a hook, you are probably on the route) to the east end of Burman Lake. (There is a log jam near the outlet stream.) Follow up the open ridge to the base of Golden Hinde, camping near a small lake on the south side of the mountain if you intend to climb it. The ascent of Golden Hinde is usually via its southeast ridge, accessed from this route by following to the east the northernmost gully above the snowfield on the south side of Golden Hinde (directly above the small lake).

i **Golden Hinde**: Vancouver Island's highest peak was known to alipinists as "The Rooster's Comb" until 1939, when it was officially named *Golden Hinde* after the ship in which Sir Francis Drake circumnavigated the globe.

Contour northwest past the small lake directly southwest of **The Behinde[i] 1989 m)** and follow the east side of the outflow stream [45]. This is a very tricky spot. The route of choice is a little exposed, and goes down, left, over the rocks before you reach the next stream. Two-thirds of the way down cut left into a shallow but reassuring crack, which returns you to the outflow stream. A long handline can be very useful here. Descend the huge snow (boulder) bowl to rejoin the direct route from Burman Lake, which we now describe.

From the meadow above the south bay of Burman Lake, contour west at the 1230 m level and follow the northwest ridge of Mount Burman to the outlet of Burman Lake. This is not as even as it appears on the map, due to granite bluffs. Alternately, work down to the southwest bay[27] and follow the shoreline to the outlet.

(e) Burman Lake to Elk River Pass (Maps B3 and A2).

Allow three days. From the west end of Burman Lake hike north, up through open areas to about the 1230 m level. Drop down a little, turn west and, at the 1200 m level, contour below the rock bluffs. Game trails and old tapes make the route fairly easy to follow where gullies must be crossed. At the heather meadows west of the Hinde, turn north at the first small lake, keeping to an open area below some rock slides [28]. A fairly level route at the 1200 m level leads to a big rockslide coming off the west (Behinde) peak.

Cross at the base of this slide and up to a saddle between Burman and Wolf River watersheds. Hike west across this and up the southeast ridge of an unnamed mountain at the head of the Ucona River. Keep to the centre of this ridge, but go to the right at one steep spot at the 1350 m level. Near the south summit, turn north. Traverse the many small summits and descend a connecting ridge to **Mount DeVoe[ii](1600 m)**. At the lowest point, go northwest, to contour around the meadows above some small lakes at 1260 m (where you can make a good camp), then north (following a creek not shown on NTS maps) up to a small col on the west ridge of Mount DeVoe. Turn sharply west up a steep heather slope to about the 1600 m level, then turn north and follow the ridge centre.

---

i   **The Behinde:** This is a local climbers' name for the peak that is two kilometres due west of the summit of the Golden Hinde.

ii **DeVoe:** According to Karl Stevenson in his *Hiking in Strathcona Park* (1974), William F. DeVoe was a member of the survey party that worked in Strathcona Park in 1913 when the Strathcona Park Act Amendment changed the boundaries of the park.

Map A2

When you are overlooking a large round lake at the head of the west fork of Wolf River, hike northwest down a side ridge to the southwest corner of this lake [29]. This is a good camping area.

The route then follows the west side of this lake across an overgrown slide area at the base of a prominent cliff, and up through a strip of timber on the south side of a small creek. Staying in the creek bed itself is a preferred option. At the top, a good game trail continues along the south side of a small lake, then northwest across flower meadows and up a final 220 m to Elk River Pass.

This ascent is steep and no clear way is obvious. Angle up with the cliffs in sight on your right in order to gain the meadows. Descending the pass, be cautious of crossing old spring snow which has been undercut by the river.

For those going south from the Elk River Pass, a special note: Your best route drops steeply down the heather before angling left, and through mature forest, towards Golden Hinde, which you can now see in the far distance. You should stay well above and to the left of a prominent rock cliff you can see directly below. It's easier if you cross creeks and stay in the forest, rather than getting into a creek gully and following it down. This section is confusing and difficult.

After the upper canyon the route follows the east side of the river, sometimes high up the side. Tape markers can usually be seen. Then come several recent avalanche debris zones. A bypass route[30] leads through one of the larger ones to the campsite on Map A2. There are two more slide zones and rock slides to negotiate, so be alert and watch for new bypass routes. Eventually you'll follow an elk trail (on the river's west side) down through the forest to the junction of the stream from Landslide Lake. The main valley trail begins here and follows the west bank of the Elk River. See (j) on page 83.

(f) Phillips Watershed High Ridge Tour
(Maps C3, B3, B4, C4)

(For access by Phillips Ridge trail from the Boliden mine site see Map C4, and description on page 57.)

Map C3

This is perhaps the most rewarding of the shorter high ridge routes, enabling the hiker with only a week to see the heart of the park. From Phillips Creek marine campsite (boat required for crossing Buttle Lake), follow the Marble Meadows trail to good camping at the 1540 m level (5-7 hours).

From here the direct route to the southwest ridge of Marble Peak bears a little right from the cairn, through a limestone section, and no height is lost. Cross the upper meadows by a good game trail to a col west of **Marble Peak (1768 m)**. By following this route, hiking traffic is directed away from the flower meadows around the lakes, already showing damage from over-use. From this col there is a choice of routes to the area of the Wheaton Hut. (To climb **Mount McBride (2081 m)** from here allow 12 hours return).

Continue down, past the hut, up the next slope a short way and contour west at about the 1540 m level, above Wheaton Lake at the head of the north fork of Phillips Creek. A wide fault leads west to a 1600 m elevation ridge. You are aiming for[31] the prominent rock spire (Morrison Spire), which dominates your immediate western skyline.

Map B3

Follow the ridge centre to a col below a waterfall coming off the main north-south ridge from McBride; (the last bump may be contoured at the 1540 m level). Go up to 1620 m, then turn south along an exposed limestone fault (with fossils) and follow this line into the col north of Limestone Cap, where there is a good campsite if you need one. From here, or even earlier, it is worth your while to hike to the summit of Morrison Spire, which is easy from the back (southwest) side. Depending on the time of day you might have your lunch on top. Limestone Cap is a flat-topped rock escarpment, deeply fissured through rainwater erosion - a fascinating place to explore. Its south slope is deep with wildflowers in spring (usually July here).

The route from here follows the divide south and is straightforward to a small, flat, east-west ridge[32], just north of a 1820 m bump. This ridge has a cliff on its south side, not shown on the NTS map, which can be avoided by contouring into the col, following an exposed ledge and gully around the west side. There are three ledges, but the one you need goes right down to the col, with a short drop at the end, where packs must be handed down (easy to find going south to north). Continue south to the 1820 m summit (which can be avoided by traversing its east side, low down) and descend, keeping to the clear ground east of the ridge's centre [33], to a large col north of **Greig Ridge[i]** (pronounced "Gregg"). Go up from this col to a good campsite at the west end of Greig Ridge, and take an easy side trip east along Greig Ridge to see the alpine flowers. The main route around the watershed continues southwest, left around a steep section near the summit and on down to a col [25] to meet with the Bedwell / Burman route.

---

i   **Greig Ridge:** Ted Greig of Royston was a hiker who took particular interest in the flowers of the area that now bears his name.

Map B4

Continue south to the west peak of Phillips Ridge (where the Bedwell route turns west), and head southeast, then follow the ridge east around the south side of the Phillips Creek watershed.

Map C4

The trail down to the Boliden mine site leaves the plateau at Arnica Lake (see page 57). Continuing east on the circuit, avoid cliffs by keeping to a ridge between creeks to gain the main south ridge of Mount Phillips.

Map C3

Hike over **Mount Phillips (1723 m)** and along the narrow north ridge. Go over the north summit (1684 m) and keep to the north ridge. At a point where the ridge becomes broken, follow a good game trail at the top of the meadows on the east side. Continue north, leaving this game trail when it veers east. At the 1230 m level take the right-hand ridge leading down to Buttle Lake at Phillips Creek. If you started your circuit from the mine site, you must now continue up the Marble Meadows Trail; see also route (h), page 53.

(g) Routes around Ralph River, Shepherd Creek and Henshaw Creek Watersheds

(Maps C3, D3, D4 and C4)

These need not be described in detail as the approaches to the main ridge route already described are quite straightforward, except for the following points:

The Delight Lake ridge route leaves the road at the north end of the Ralph River bridge. Cross a log jam at the junction of Shepherd Creek and Ralph River.[i] The next section is bushy through a burn and the forest here is almost impenetrable, thick hemlock; keep within the sound of Shepherd Creek until you reach unburned timber, then angle back to the left, staying in old-growth as much as possible until past the burn. Near the timberline, bear right to avoid cliffs.

Map D3

This is a good alternate way to Comox Glacier, leading up to the main route above Ink Lake. Contour across the triangular glacier north of Ink Lake and up its east side to gain the main ridge [5].

---

[i] **Ralph River:** William Ralph was in charge of surveying the western boundary of the E & N Railway Land Grant (later the eastern boundary of Strathcona Park) in 1892.

Map C3

The route up the ridge between Shepherd and Henshaw Creeks leaves the road at the creek, which enters above a small bay 2.8 km south of the Ralph River campground.

Map C4

Start up on the right side of the creek following a game trail, alongside a rock bluff, to a more open area under some mature forest. Staying on the south side of the creek, continue southeast up to the centre of the ridge. It is clear going under old-growth to the alpine zone, but keep clear of an old burn near Shepherd Creek.

Maps C4, D4

The summit ridge involves some climbing, but this can be avoided (given safe conditions) by contouring across the snow slope to the glacier. An alternative route credited to Albert Hestler avoids snow slopes but adds some steep hiking. It leaves the main route at [37] to drop down to the lake, regaining the main route at [38]. After the summit, contour across glaciers to pass north of Tzela Lake.

(h) Augerpoint Route to Mount Albert Edward
(Maps C3, D2)

A difficult route, only suitable for experienced hikers. The route has been marked right across with cairns, but the area is subject to considerable changes from year to year and cairns are often covered with snow well into the summer. From the foot of the ridge, at the Buttle Lake roadside, to the first good campsite takes about 2 hours, and 5 hours to the upper lakes. See also (b), page 52.

Map D2

From **Ruth Masters Lake**[i] there are cairns along the sometimes hard-to-locate route until you come to the foot of the south ridge leading to Mount Albert Edward. There is only one place to get up, staying as far to the right as possible (but it is not signed or marked with cairns). Conversely, if going from Mount Albert Edward, turn west on the long ridge and go down off it, but there is only one place to go down (not signed). Note: there is an 853 m elevation advantage if you hike this route westward from Paradise Meadows.

---

i   **Ruth Masters Lake:** Ruth Masters has been instrumental in getting many of the local place-names made official. We are indebted to her for supplying us with background information on the place-names that appear in this section of the book. In Ruth's inimitable style she writes, "Ruth Masters Lake and Syd Watts Peak are lined up on their [Mapping Branch] maps to become official two years after Syd and I go upstairs."

(i) Drinkwater Creek to Price Creek (Map C5)

From the north end of Della Falls trail, the route to the head of the Drinkwater Creek valley goes through a slide area. Pick your way up, taking advantage of gravel bars where possible. Travel is mostly up the creek bed itself, especially the last half-kilometre up to the waterfall. This section is extremely difficult. It is not possible to avoid the water, so be prepared for wet feet. Where the valley turns northwest, keep to the right of the waterfall and then follow the valley's centre to Drinkwater Pass, usually on snow. Here you join the main route described between Cream Lake and Bedwell Lake, and the route from Price Creek described in (c) this section, page 72.

(j) Elk River Trail south to Elk River Pass
(Maps A1 and A2).

Slides impede many parts of the upper Elk River Valley. Some slides occurred in the spring of 1999, as a result of the heavy snows over the previous winter; others are more recent. Avalanche debris obscures the regular trail and chokes the river in spots, with logs and trees pushed well up the opposite embankment. Follow bypass routes in these areas.

From the gravel flats a kilometre below Landslide Lake, cross a bridge to the east side of the creek coming down from Landslide Lake. The elk trail enters the forest about 100 m up the west bank of the Elk River. Following the valley in a southeastwardly direction, this clearly defined trail eventually reaches the first of several avalanche paths.

Once you reach the debris don't be tempted to cross to the east side (the left bank, looking upstream) of the river on the first log jam you come to. Look for flagging marking a bypass route leading up to a ledge that parallels the river on its west side (the right bank, looking upstream). Continue until you reach impassable cliffs, then drop down to the riverbed and cut over to the east side on avalanche debris. Stay low near the river bottom until you are past the mess. The slide zone is almost continuous for 200 m until you hit the big timber where one can easily pick up the elk trail that leads to the excellent campsite in a stand of trees on the river's east side.

Beyond this, find your way about 300 m through thick slide alder growing over a rockslide from Elkhorn Mountain. Here you'll encounter more avalanche debris. Rather than follow the river, go as far as possible into the big timber and look for flagging leading into slide alder. Someone has gone in with a chainsaw to make this bypass route [30] easier. Traverse southwest across several slides, gullies and bands of trees, back to the river.

When clear of the canyon, angle down to the stream and cross the Elk River from the east side to the west to avoid an impassable section upstream. Traverse the west side of the river, above some steep bluffs, and rejoin the river after about 500 m. From here the valley floor is open. Generally follow the east side of the creek leading to the pass. See (e) on page 78.

(k) Elkhorn Mountain Access Route (Map A1)

Follow the Elk River Trail for 2½ km (about an hour) and cross the river (on a tricky log crossing) to where the route begins on the south side of a prominent creek. This route to the northwest ridge is fairly obvious and flagged in places. Stay to the right at steep sections. Most groups with full packs will take six to seven hours to reach the usual campsite (see map A1). On a clear day you'll be able to see Elkhorn Mountain, Vancouver Island's second highest peak, and Kings Peak and Victoria Peak. From the campsite it is 4 to 5 hours to the summit. Camping here leaves enough time to hike out to your car that same day. The route to the summit of **Elkhorn Mountain (2195 m)** is not for hikers unless they are also rock climbers. There is lots of exposure, loose rock, possible rappels and intricate route finding - serious stuff. Caution is required, and the assurance of a climbing rope.

Colonel Foster

The Golden Hinde from Burman Lake

Septimus

Elkhorn

Strathcona Provincial Park
Key To Maps

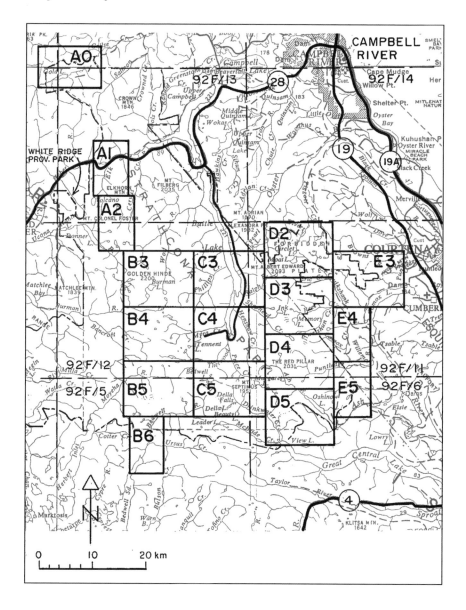

Map A1 Elk River

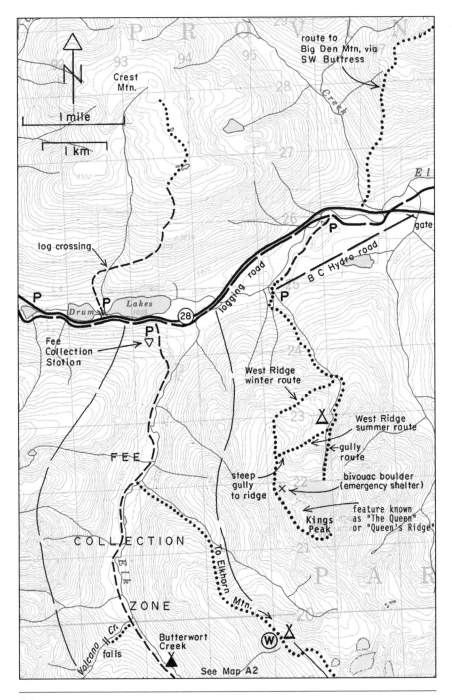

Map A2 Landslide Lake

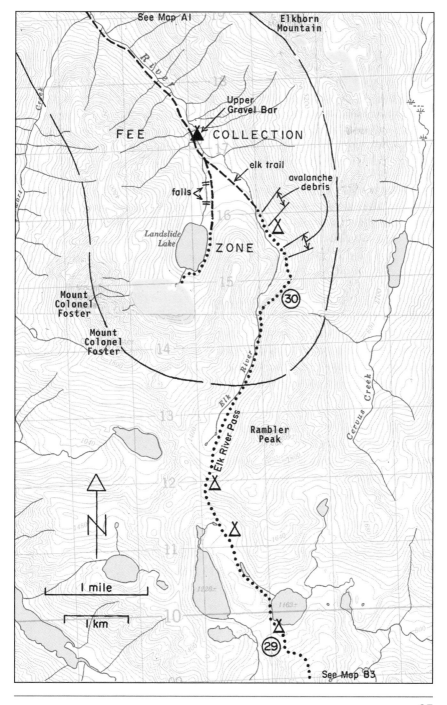

Map B3 **Golden Hinde**

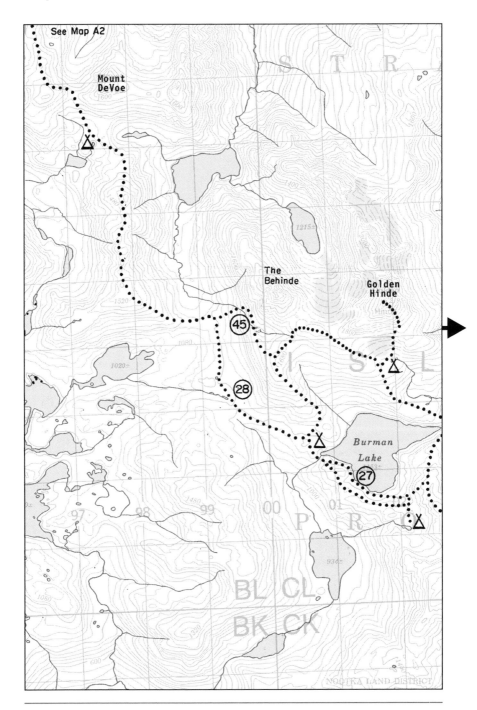

Map B3 **Golden Hinde**

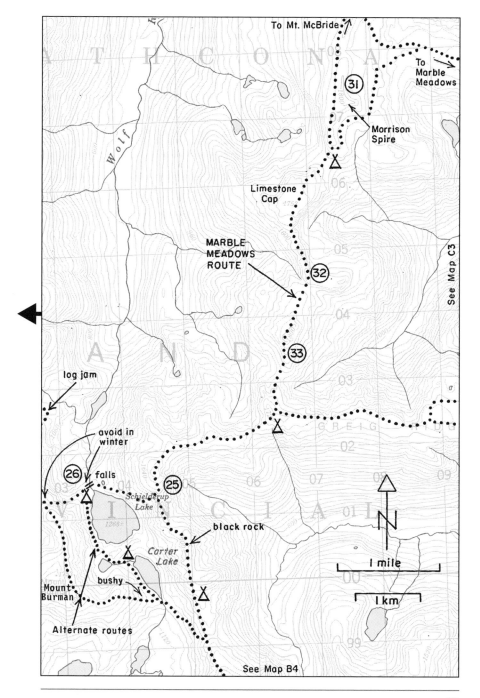

Map B4 Mount Thelwood

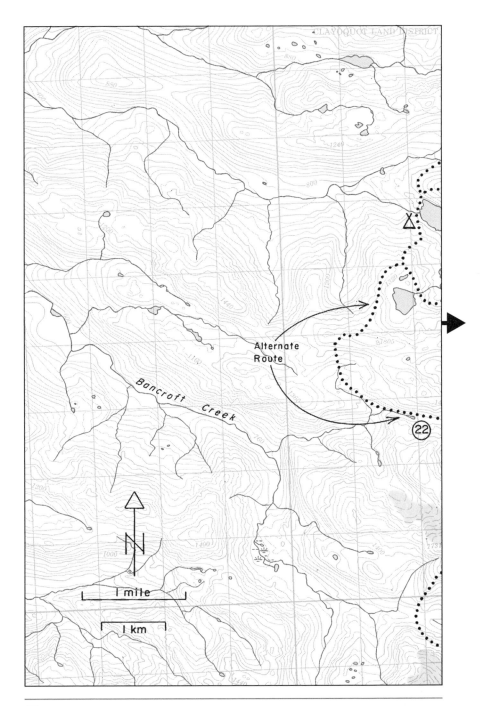

Map B4 **Mount Thelwood**

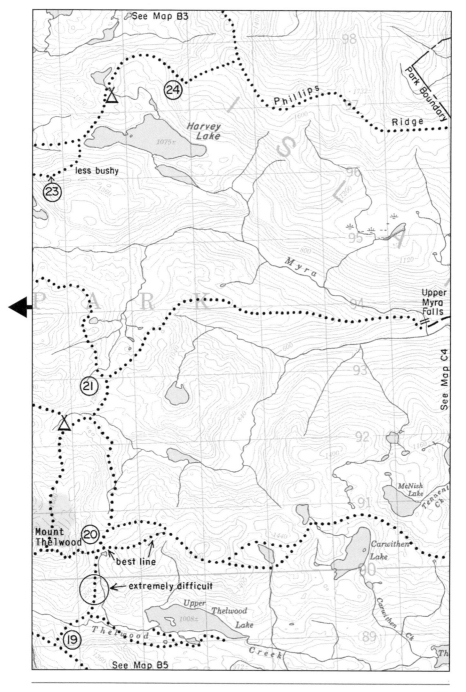

Map B5 **Bedwell River**

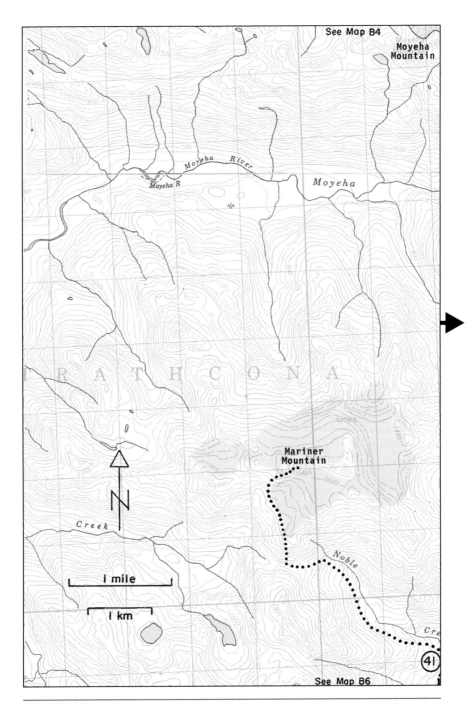

Map B5 Bedwell River

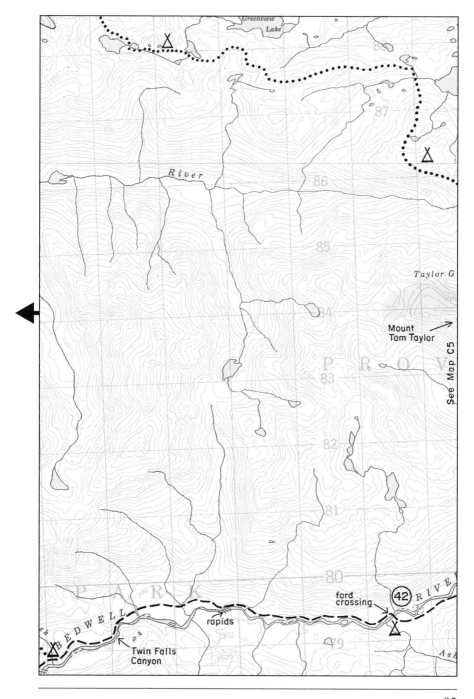

Map B6 **Bedwell Sound**

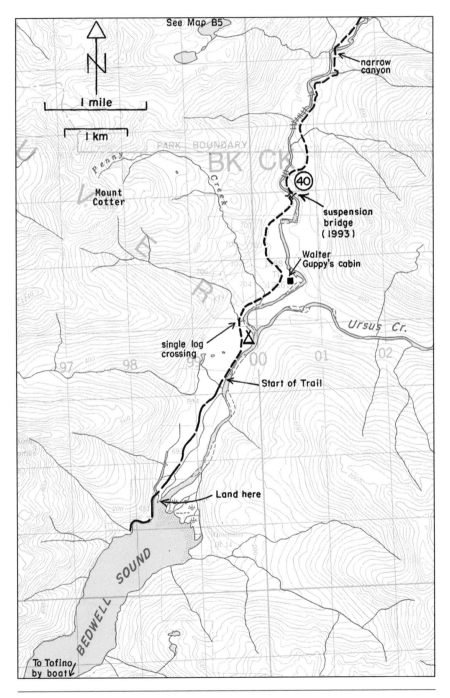

Baby Bedwell Lake. See pages 55 and 74.

Thelwood Creek, near the head of Buttle Lake and the start of the Price Creek Trail. See page 54.

Map C3 **Buttle Lake**

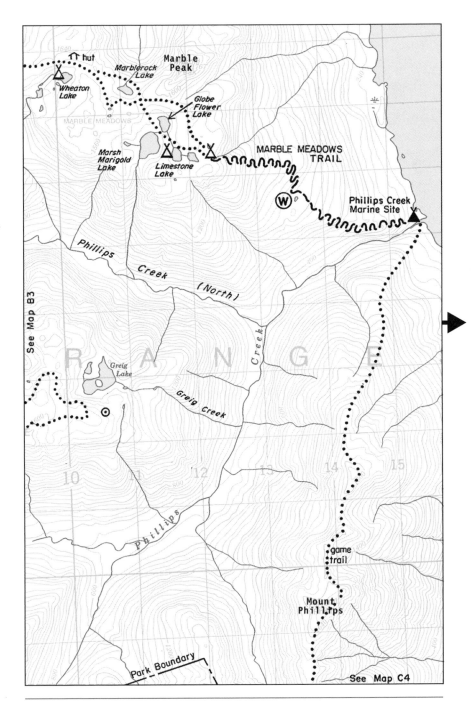

Map C3 Buttle Lake

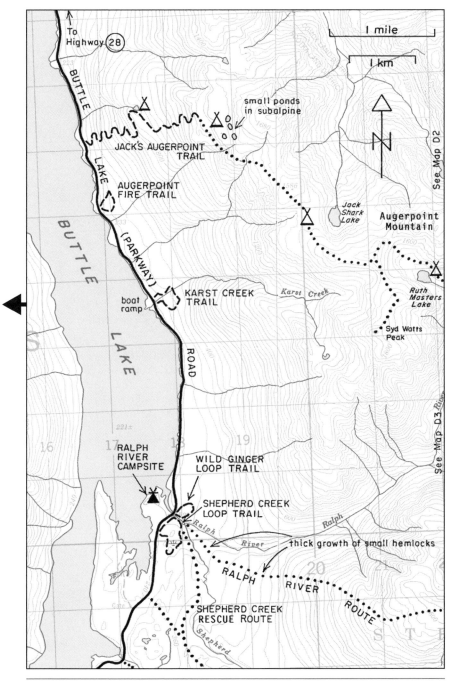

Map C4 **Flower Ridge**

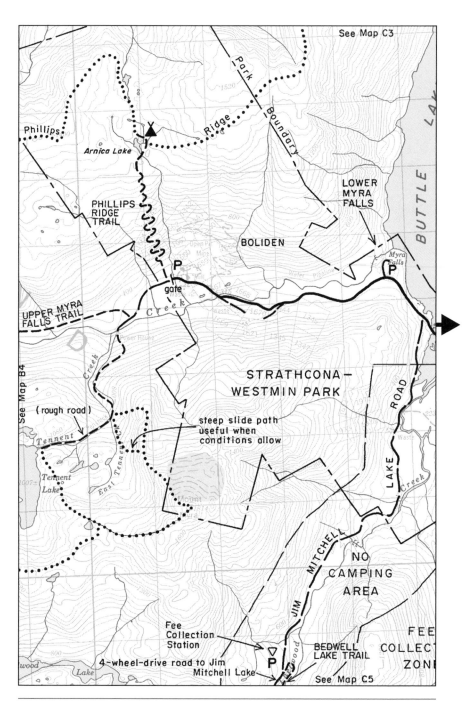

Map C4 **Flower Ridge**

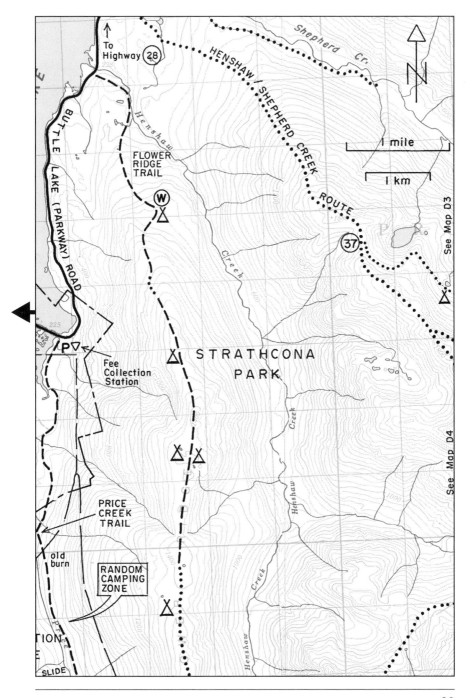

Map C5 Della Falls

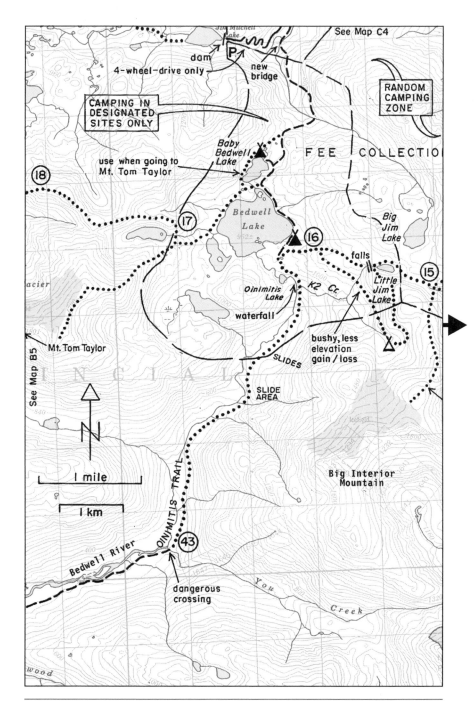

Map C5 Della Falls

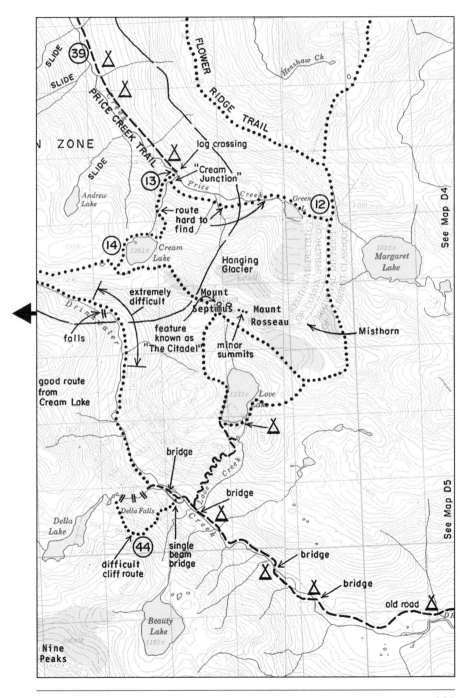

Map D2 **Paradise Meadows**

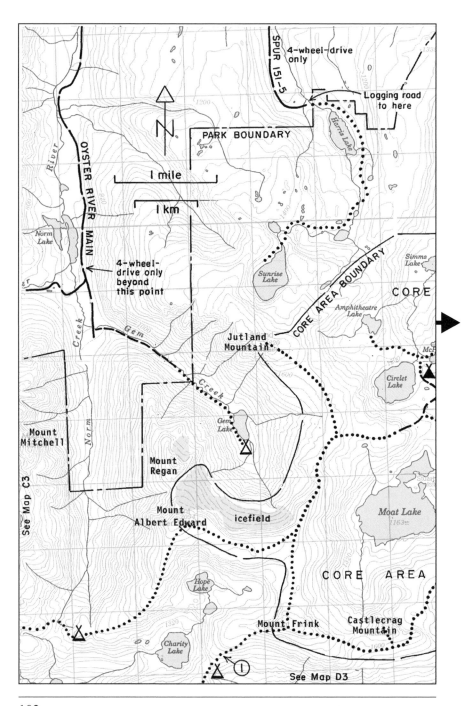

Map D2 Paradise Meadows

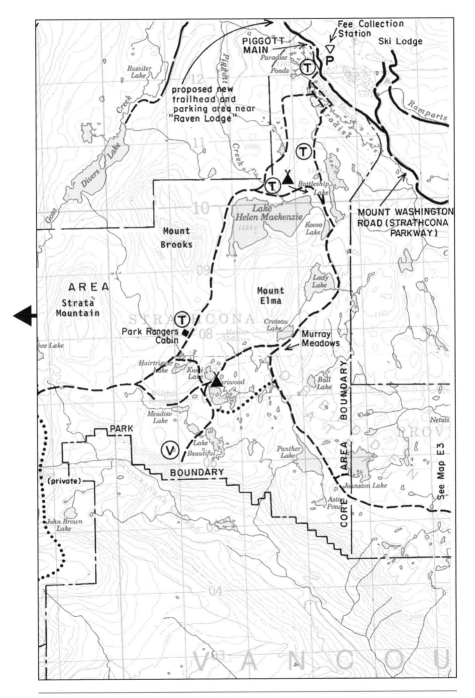

Map D3 **Rees Ridge**

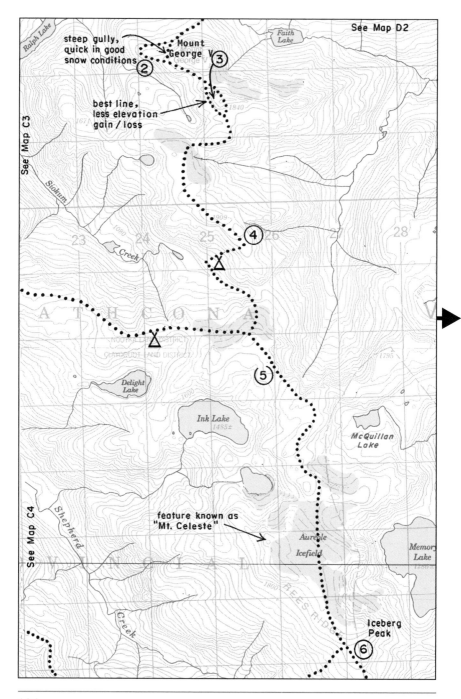

Map D3 Rees Ridge

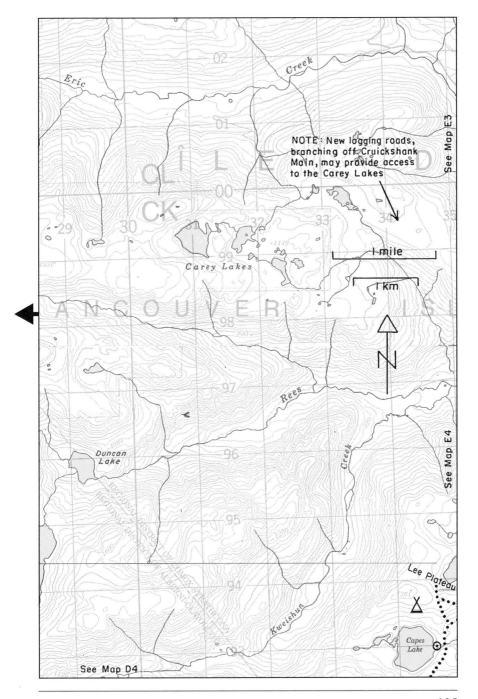

NOTE: New logging roads, branching off Cruickshank Main, may provide access to the Carey Lakes

Map D4 **Comox Glacier**

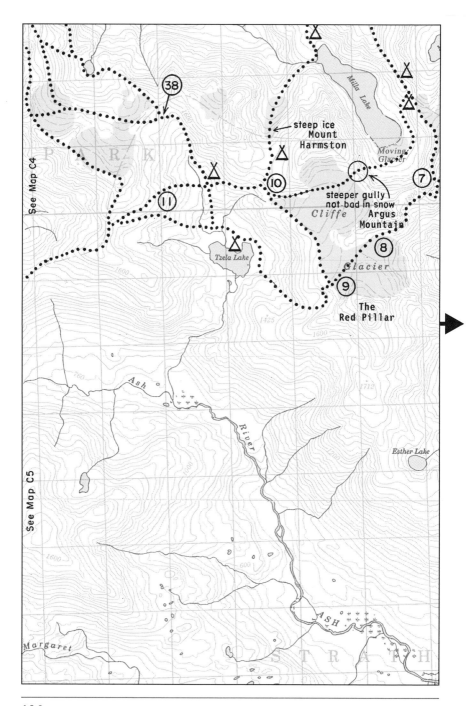

Map D4 **Comox Glacier**

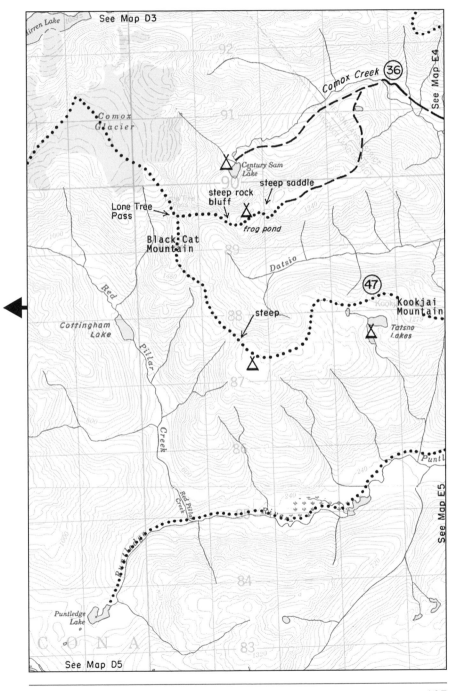

Map D5 Oshinow Lake

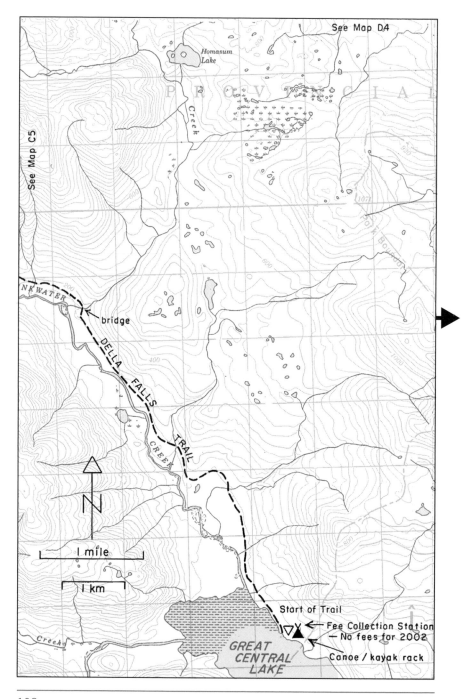

Map D5 Oshinow Lake

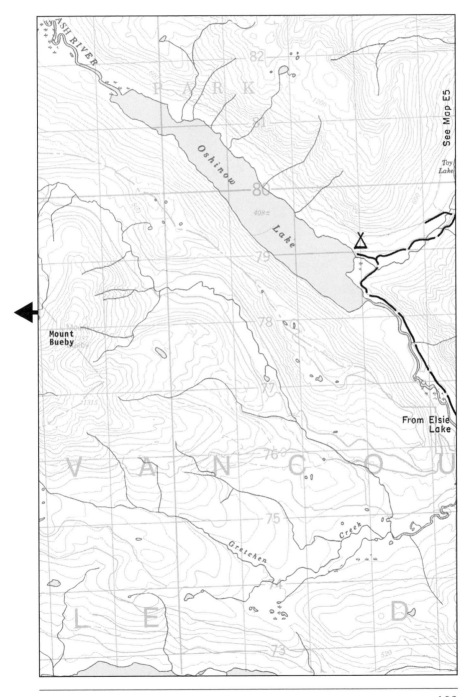

Map E3 **Forbidden Plateau**

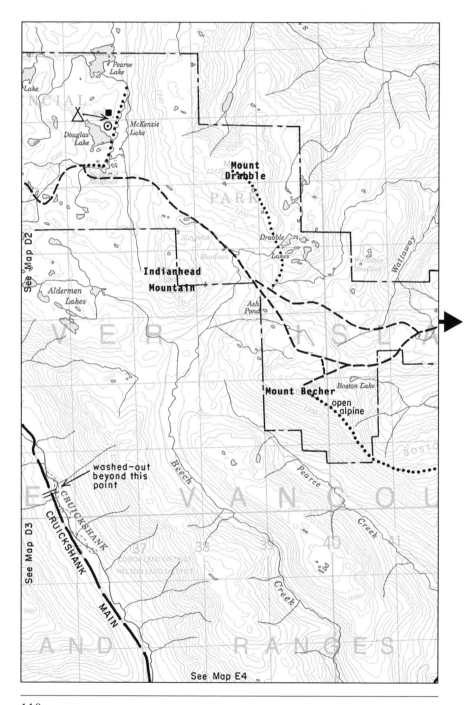

Map E3 **Forbidden Plateau**

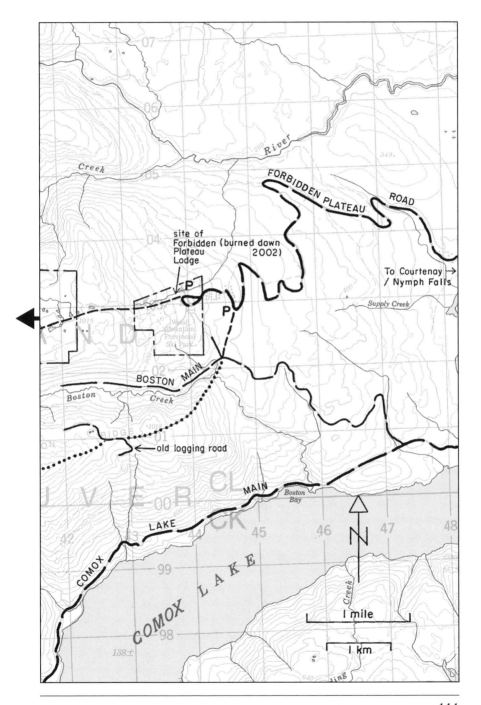

Map E4 Comox Creek

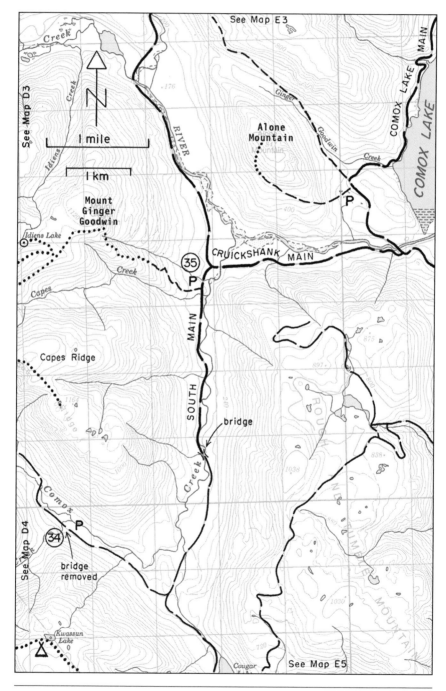

Map E5 Willemar/Forbush Lakes

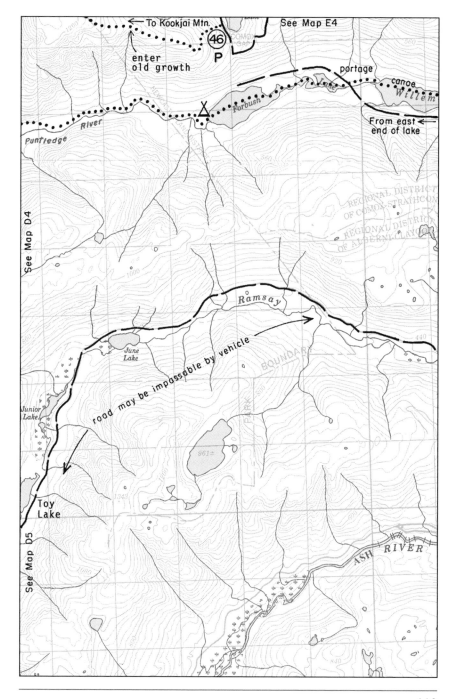

Section 3

Other Areas

1. Clayoquot Sound and Western Strathcona Provincial Park

(Map 1, page 118)

Clayoquot Sound has been the ancestral home of the Nuu-chah-nulth for thousands of years. Included are the Ahousaht, the Hesquiaht and Tla-o-qui-aht First Nations. When exploring this spectacular region, respect their traditional territories. There are numerous Indian Reserves in Clayoquot Sound. Please do not visit these sites without permission.

(a) **Clayoquot Arm Provincial Park (3490 ha)** protects habitat for spawning salmon and an old-growth Sitka spruce forest near Kennedy Lake's Clayoquot Arm.

(b) **Clayoquot Plateau Provincial Park (3155 ha)** features sinkholes and limestone caves and an old-growth forest on a high elevation plateau.

(c) **Cleland Island Ecological Reserve (no public access)** lies west of Vargas Island (within Vargas Island Park) and protects important marine habitat for water birds. The reserve includes Cleland Island and a marine area with a 10 km radius around the island.

(d) **Dawley Passage Provincial Park (154 ha)** on Meares Island's south side has a varied marine ecosystem and nearby channels are subject to strong tideflows, particularly Fortune Channel.

(e) **Epper Passage Provincial Park (306 ha)** encompasses two small islands (Morfee and Dunlap) in the marine rich waters just east of Vargas Island.

(f) **Flores Island Provincial Park (7113 ha)** preserves three pristine watersheds and their adjacent old-growth Sitka spruce forests. The park has spectacular rocky shorelines and sandy beaches. Island wolves may frequent campsites in the early morning, late evening and at night. Ensure your food is secure. Do not feed the island's wolves. This is a violation of the Parks Act.

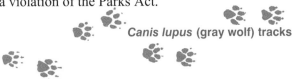

Canis lupus (gray wolf) tracks

(g) **Gibson Provincial Marine Park (140 ha)** at the south end of Flores Island, in Matilda Inlet, is known for the Ahousat Warm Springs and the beautiful beaches of Whitesand Cove.

(h) **Hesquiat Lake Provincial Park (62 ha)** protects a stand of shoreline forest near Hesquiat Lake, north of Hesquiat Harbour.

(i) **Hesquiat Peninsula Provincial Park (7888 ha)** includes pockets of old-growth forest, shorelines and offshore reefs.

(j) **Kennedy River Bog Provincial Park (11 ha)** preserves a bog near the Kennedy River that has unusually low acidity.

(k) **Maquinna Provincial Marine Park (2667 ha)**, near Hot Springs Cove, has natural hot springs. Change houses and toilets are provided. No soap, shampoo, alcohol, glass, pets, or camping at the hot springs.

(l) **Megin River Ecological Reserve (no public access)** and the **Megin / Talbot addition (27,391 ha)** in western Strathcona Provincial Park include a pristine watershed. The area features **karst**[i] topography, old-growth forests and valuable salmon habitat.

Kennedy Lake

i   See footnote page 186.

(m) **Pacific Rim National Park Reserve** has many trails in the Long Beach area. For information and a detailed brochure contact Pacific Rim National Park Reserve, P.O. Box 280, 2185 Ocean Terrace Road, Ucluelet, BC V0R 3A0 (250) 726-7721; (250) 726-4720 (fax); Long Beach Information Centre (250) 726-4212 (seasonal). *Hiking Trails II: South-Central Vancouver Island and the Gulf Islands* contains descriptions of the trails in this region.

Ucluelet's *Wild Pacific Trail*, a planned 17 km trail between Ucluelet and Halfmoon Bay, in Pacific Rim National Park Reserve, is an ongoing project of the Wild Pacific Trail Society. This non-profit organization has already completed about 8.5 km of this striking coastal route. It stretches from Ucluelet's He-Tin-Kis Park to a point along the highway. Inspired by local resident "Oyster Jim" Martin, the trail has been developed with donated funds and hours of volunteer work. Contact the WPTS c/o Box 48, Ucluelet, BC V0R 3A0 or visit: www.wildpacifictrail.com for further information.

(n) **Sulphur Passage Provincial Park (2299 ha)** includes the scenic channel between Obstruction and Flores islands, the nearby estuary and old-growth forests. This is an important salmon habitat.

(o) **Sydney Inlet Provincial Park (2774 ha)** protects the fjord (Sydney Inlet) and its old-growth forest. The area is a valuable salmon habitat.

(p) **Tranquil Creek Provincial Park (Paradise Lake) (299 ha)**, near the headwaters of Tranquil Creek, includes untouched Paradise Lake and its surrounding alpine meadows and forests.

(q) **Vargas Island Provincial Park (5970 ha)** features beautiful sandy beaches, a protected lagoon and a rugged, open coastline.

The BC Parks brochure for **Clayoquot Sound Provincial Park** has a map and valuable travel hints. Copies are usually available at local tourist infocentres but may run out.

NOTES:

Suspension bridge over the Big Qualicum River, Horne Lake Caves Provincial Park. See page 120.

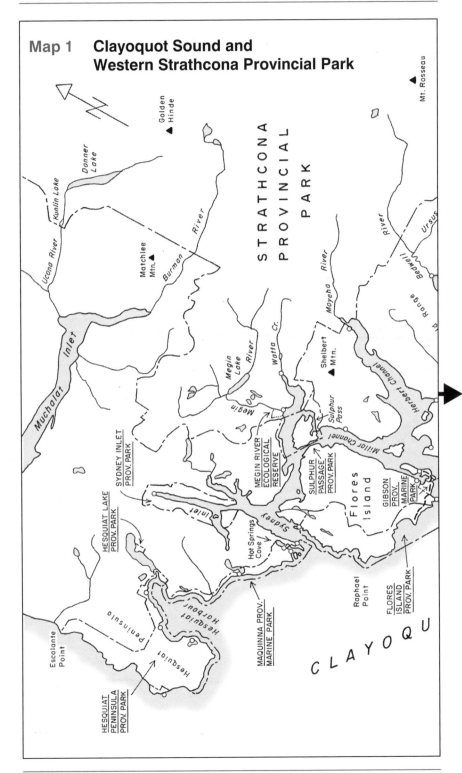

Map 1 Clayoquot Sound and Western Strathcona Provincial Park

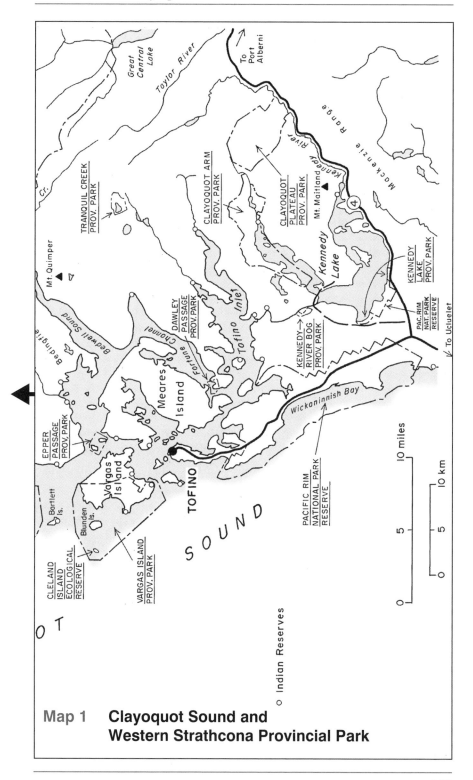

Map 1   Clayoquot Sound and Western Strathcona Provincial Park

2. The Beaufort Range

(Map 2A, page 121/Map 2B, page 123)

Extending from Horne Lake[i] in the south to Cumberland in the north, the Beaufort Range[ii] has been well used by members of the Comox District Mountaineering Club. Over the years the club has cleared some of the overgrown logging roads and built trails to some of the most beautiful places on the range. Accessed near Fanny Bay and the Rosewall Creek area via the Horne/Bowser Forest Service Road (FSR), **Mount Joan (1557 m)** (the highest mountain in the Beaufort Range) and **Mount Curran (1478 m)** have established trails. Further to the north trails have been created on **Mount Clifton (1420 m)** and **Mount Chief Frank (1470 m)**.

Rosewall Creek Provincial Park (54 ha), close to the highway turnoff, features a picturesque 2 km trail along Rosewall Creek to a waterfall. There is a wheelchair path here.

To the south, near Horne Lake, **Horne Lake Regional Park (105.3 ha)** was officially opened in July 2002. Close to **Horne Lake Caves Provincial Park**, the new park will eventually be connected by regional trails to Port Alberni and the east coast of Vancouver Island. For more information contact the Regional District of Nanaimo at (250) 752-7199.

(a) Mount Joan Trail (Map 2A, page 121)

From the new Inland Island Highway (Highway 19), turn west at the lights at the Cook Road intersection, near Fanny Bay. At the T-junction turn left onto the gravel logging road and follow it 2 km to the next junction. Take the right fork down the bank (not Chef Main to the left). From the highway drive 14 km and take the right fork just before the bridge that crosses Rosewall Creek. There is limited parking nearby. The road becomes accessible only for four-wheel-drive vehicles after this point. The road begins climbing and goes through a nasty cross ditch filled with logs. After this the road continues up several switchbacks to a major corner. Either park at the corner or for the more adventurous drive up the left fork towards Mount Joan. Be advised that this road is very rough and difficult to turn a vehicle around on.

The trail begins following the old logging road. After a short distance in a little alder clearing, signs indicate the **trail junction for Mount Joan and Mount Curran**. For Mount Joan follow the sign and trail to the left to a major washout at Roaring Creek. The trail descends to the creek then up a

---

i   Adam Horne (1831-1903) discovered the lake in 1856.

ii Sir Francis Beaufort (1774-1857) was a hydrographer with the Royal Navy.

Map 2A **Mount Joan / Mount Curran**

Note: Contour lines are at 100–metre intervals.

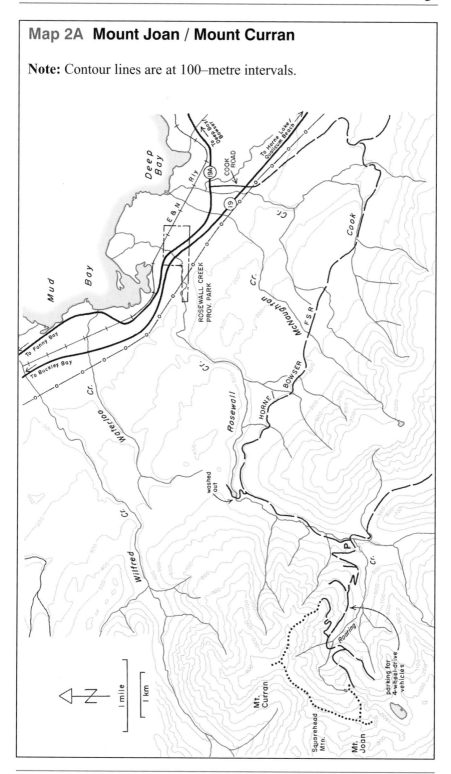

steep bank on the other side. Continue up the logging road as it switchbacks higher. The trail veers off up the bank to the right through a clearcut and into the old-growth trees on the left-hand side. The trail steepens to a little saddle overlooking small tarns in a basin below Mount Joan and Square-head Mountain. From the tarns follow the small creek into the upper meadows and up a spur onto the ridge just to the north of Mount Joan. On the summit is a radio repeater tower. An easy 1.2 km ridge walk to the north leads to the summit of Squarehead Mountain. Mount Curran is accessible from Squarehead Mountain and requires climbing down into the interven-ing saddle and then up a steep ridge, which leads to some small tarns on Mount Curran's summit ridge.

(b) Mount Curran Trail   (Map 2A, page 121)

From the Mount Joan / Mount Curran junction in the alder clearing (see Mount Joan Trail description above) veer right up the logging road and follow several switchbacks to the end of the road. On the left the trail climbs through some second-growth into a small patch of old-growth and into an old burned area on the southeast ridge. Eventually the trail exits the burn and enters the forest, then the sub-alpine area. The trail becomes harder to see but look for flagging in the trees and rock cairns higher up. Once in the alpine follow the ridge to the north past several inviting tarns to a wide-open summit.

(c) Mount Clifton Trail   (Map 2B, page 123)

From the lights on Highway 19 (Inland Island Highway) at the Buckley Bay/Denman Island ferry intersection turn inland up Buckley Bay Main. **There is a gate on the logging road near the highway that is locked except during hunting season (October to December) when someone from Weyerhaeuser works the gate. Expect a $2 access fee. There is a second gate at the 14 km mark that is usually locked. Most of the time it is necessary to phone Weyerhaeuser's Northwest Bay Division in advance to get the key.** (See *Logging Companies* on page 24.) Hiking clubs, schools and other groups can also arrange for a key at other times of the year.

Continue along Buckley Bay Main past Sheila Lake Main to the sign that says "Lunchtime Lake" to the left. The road heads around the north side of the lake. A high-slung four-wheel-drive vehicle is required beyond Lunch-time Lake. About half a kilometre beyond the lake a road to the left crosses the creek and starts winding up towards Kim Lake, which is tucked in behind a small hill. At the end of the road (about 1 km) pick up the flagged trail to Kim Lake. The trail heads around the north side of the lake and then climbs a steep, northeast-sloping spur. Once in the alpine the summit is about 400 m to the west. There is a well-built cairn on the summit and a register.

Map 2B Mount Clifton / Mount Chief Frank

Note: Contour lines are at 40–metre intervals

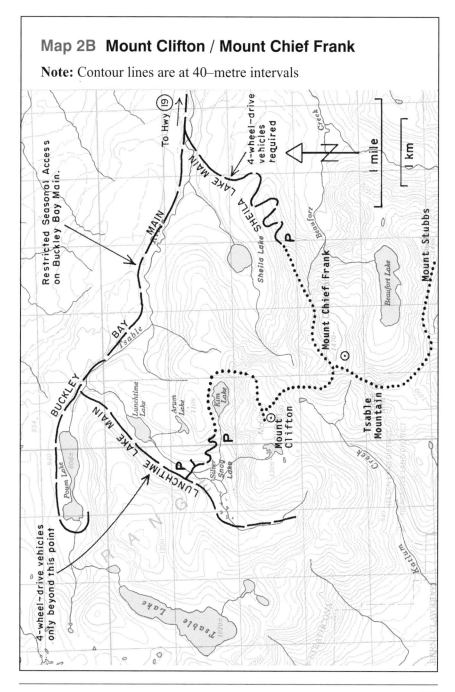

(d) Mount Chief Frank Trail (Map 2B, page 123)

See Section (c), page 122. The route to the trail for Mount Chief Frank also turns off the Island Highway at the intersection at Buckley Bay and follows Buckley Bay Main. At the 16 km mark turn left onto Sheila Lake Main and cross the Tsable River. You will need a high-slung four-wheel-drive vehicle to make it all the way to the trailhead. Take the second left and follow small rock cairns that have been placed on the side of the road at each corner to indicate which road to take.

The trail begins high on the ridge at a turnaround at the end of the road. Initially the trail is not well defined as it climbs through big old-growth timber but watch for flagging tape on the trees. At 1100 m the trail becomes obvious as it climbs through a narrow section of the ridge and up a short, steep little bluff. Above this the trail continues up to the base of the bluffs at 1240m.

There are two routes up to the summit. The first (and most frequently used) route angles up the benches under the north face and around to the northwest side of the mountain. Ascend through easy heather benches onto the summit ridge and angle east for 500 m to the summit. A large rock cairn, with a register, is on the summit. The second route cuts out to the left at the base of the bluffs. Drop down into the head of a small creek and climb up the other side. Continue working your way under the bluffs to another small creek. Cross this stream then get out onto a small spur that leads onto heather slopes and then angles up to the summit. This route is not flagged but makes for an interesting traverse of the mountain.

(e) Mount Clifton to Mount Joan High Level Traverse (not shown on our maps)

Although this traverse is rarely climbed and is not well flagged, it is a beautiful high-level traverse of the Beaufort Range. Beginning at the trailhead for Mount Clifton follow the trail past Kim Lake and up to the summit of the mountain. Descend the south side to a saddle at the head of Katlum Creek and then up onto Mount Chief Frank. It is not necessary to go to the summit as the route descends through steep bluffs to the southwest to a saddle between Mount Chief Frank and Tsable Mountain. It is an easy climb up to the summit of Tsable Mountain where there is a repeater tower. Look for carvings on some of the trees with the names and dates of the surveyors from the 1940s. From the top of Tsable Mountain the route continues to the south along a wide spur over to Mount Stubbs. There are no established campsites along this route but there are numerous small tarns that are idyllic to camp beside.

From the top of Mount Stubbs descend south of the mountain and follow the ridge towards Mount Henry Spencer. Don't expect to find any flagging on this part of the route. From Mount Henry Spencer follow the ridge to the southeast going up and down numerous small mountains until Mount Apps is reached at the head of Tumblewater Creek. Descend south of the summit onto a wide meadow with lots of little tarns and ponds. This is another beautiful place to camp.

Continue south out of the meadows and into the forest, then down to a saddle at the head of Wilfred Creek (1190 m). Now begins the climb up the northwest spur to the summit of Squarehead Mountain. From Squarehead Mountain climb over to Mount Joan and from the trail there, down to the logging roads and trailhead.

Beaufort Range material contributed by
Lindsay Elms and Ken Rodonets

Lindsay Elms is the author of ***Beyond Nootka: A Historical Perspective of Vancouver Island Mountains***, published by Misthorn Press. For information visit www.island.net/~ekerr/.

Amor Lake is one of several making up the Sayward Forest Canoe Route. See page 162.

3. Seal Bay Regional Nature Park (Xwee Xwhwa Luq)

(Map 3, page 127)

Xwee Xwhwa Luq is a Salish name suggested by the Comox Band meaning, "place with an atmosphere of peace and serenity". Situated near Seal Bay, just 15 minutes north of Courtenay or Comox, the original trails were constructed between 1971 and 1973 by the Comox Valley Naturalists Society with LIP grant support. Seasonal trail maintenance is done mainly by volunteers. Please respect their continuing efforts.

Newcomers are recommended to access the park at the main parking area, on Bates Road, coming in via Anderton or Coleman roads. Other access points are Clark, Elmo, Fitzell, Hardy, Huband, Loxley, Seabank and Seacliff roads.

The park has 25 km of trails, including some new bike/horse trails on the perimeter. Yellow markers indicate these multi-use trails. The core area is for hikers only. No camping, hunting, fires or motorized vehicles are allowed. Remember to leash all dogs. Pack out what you carry in. The park is closed from 11 pm to 6:30 am. Trails may be slippery in heavy rains or hazardous during high winds due to falling branches and trees. Be cautious near the ravines and keep well back from undercut banks.

Seal Bay Regional Park is administered as a nature park by the Regional District of Comox-Strathcona. Of its 714 ha, the Crown Land portion (564 ha) is managed under a Licence of Occupation.

NOTES:

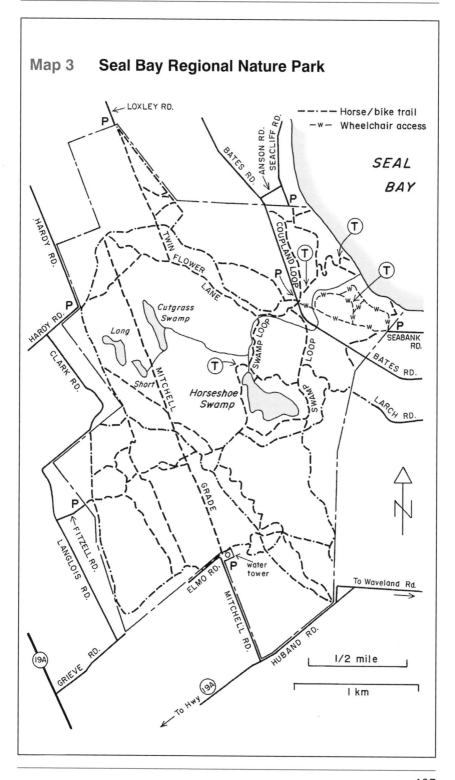

Map 3   Seal Bay Regional Nature Park

4. Quadra Island
(Map 4A, page 130 / Map 4B, page 136)

Quadra Island[i] is a short ferry ride across Discovery Passage from Campbell River. Here, just over two hundred years ago, Captain Vancouver made contact with the aboriginal people. He sent yawls (a type of small boat) through Discovery Passage before he brought in his ship, "Discovery", and anchored off **Cape Mudge**[ii]. Today the village of We-Wai-kai offers visitors a modern museum displaying outstanding examples of aboriginal art, returned from Ottawa where they had been held since confiscated by the RCMP in 1921.

The island offers many recreational opportunities including coastal kayaking, diving and fishing, lake canoeing and kayaking, and hiking. Although some trails are long established, others have only been made recently, and many are former logging grades. On Quadra, as throughout BC, choices are being made as to how and where recreational opportunities, such as trails, will be developed.

The trails and routes described below are located in the northern central part of Quadra Island, with road distances measured from Heriot Bay store. All the *trails* are maintained locally by volunteers and are well signed. *Routes*, which are passable ways that may not be maintained or signed, are usually only suitable for experienced hikers.

Generally these trails and routes are located on Crown land, which is managed by the Ministry of Forests and/or TimberWest, the forest company holding Tree Farm License (TFL) #47. We acknowledge their assistance and co-operation in constructing these trails. The kindness of private-land-owners, in permitting trails and routes over their land, is also very much appreciated.

Quadra Island Notes:
Substantial changes to Quadra Island's trails have occurred since the last edition of *Hiking Trails III* was published. Some of these are due to the effects of increased logging and wood lot activities, and the resultant access road and trail modifications. In other areas, some routes have been upgraded from routes to trails and their official status now reflects this new classification.

---

i   **Quadra Island** is named after Don Juan Francisco de la Bodega y Quadra, a Spanish naval officer who explored the west coast in 1775 and 1779.

ii Captain Vancouver named the cape in 1792, after his first lieutenant on HMS *Discovery*, Zachary **Mudge** (1770-1852).

The provincial government has recently (2002) abdicated responsibility for upkeep of BC's forest trails. To ensure these assets are not lost to the public, volunteers are donating a lot of time to maintaining official "gazetted" trails, which is why many remain open. On Quadra Island, a number of these volunteers previously enjoyed going beyond the bounds of the more popular trails. They regularly used routes, which, as a result, were maintained to some degree. This shift in priorities means some routes are, in turn, now being neglected.

During the winter of 2001/2002, a series of unprecedented windstorms caused extensive blowdowns, which seriously impacted trails throughout Quadra Island. Repairing them has placed even more burden on the limited volunteer resource.

There has been a large increase in the amount of logging taking place on Quadra Island. This often affects trails and routes, as well as access to them. Real effort has been made to provide accurate information at the time of writing, but subsequent industrial activity can easily alter the situation on the ground. Readers should be aware the descriptions and directions given here might be affected by such operations.

Noel Lax, and fellow hikers of Quadra Island

Morte Lake Area

From the Heriot Bay store, take the Hyacinthe Bay Road for 6.1 km to Walcan Road. Turn west (left) along it for 750 m to the Morte Lake parking area.

(a) Morte Lake Trail: South Shore Loop
(Map 4B, page 136)

This is a pleasant forest hike of 7.2 km with good views of Morte Lake, the southwest slopes of the Chinese Mountains and glimpses of the mountains of Vancouver Island. Travelling in a counter-clockwise direction the trail follows a gentle incline above McKercher Creek for 2.3 km to the east end of Morte Lake, which takes about 30 minutes. Stay to the left at the fork just before (east of) the lake, and follow the trail to a small marshy area (bridged) by a sandy beach at the southernmost end of the lake. The trail rises again over rock ridges before dropping steeply to Mud Lake. At times the Mud Lake and Reed Lake sections can be wet, and if so, the Walcan Road may be accessed from the west end of each of these lakes. Allow about two hours, return.

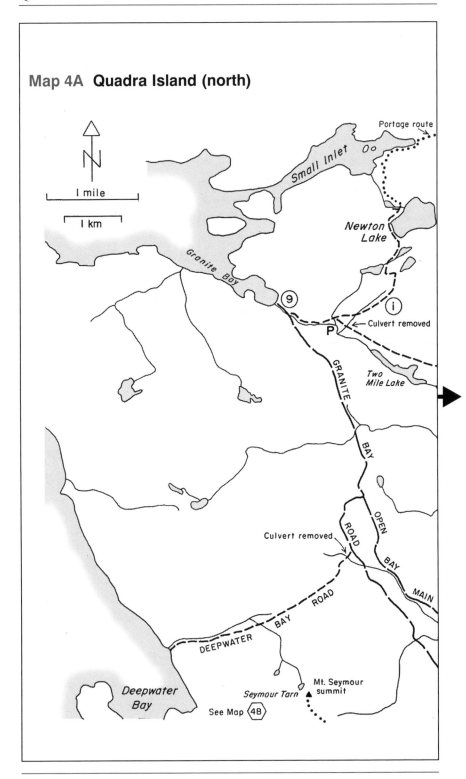

Map 4A **Quadra Island (north)**

Map 4A Quadra Island (north)

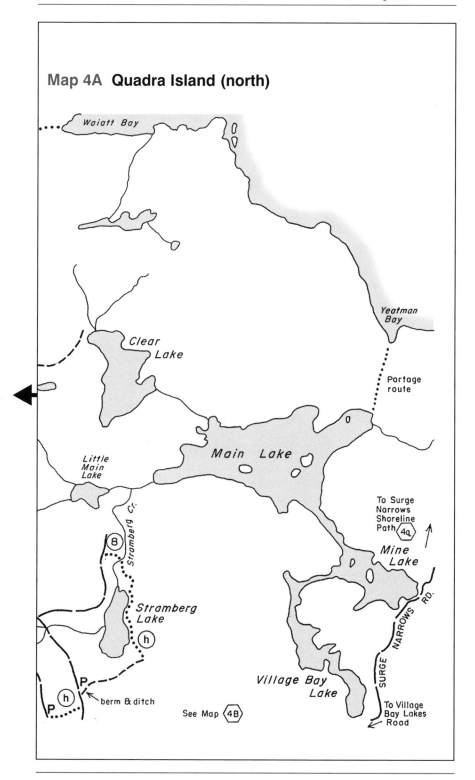

Waiatt Bay

Yeatman Bay

Clear Lake

Portage route

Little Main Lake

Main Lake

0

To Surge Narrows Shoreline Path ⟨4a⟩

Stramberg Cr.

⟨8⟩

Mine Lake

Stramberg Lake

ⓗ

P

ⓗ

P

berm & ditch

Village Bay Lake

See Map ⟨4B⟩

SURGE NARROWS RD.

To Village Bay Lakes Road

(b) Morte Lake Trail: North Shore

(Map 4B, page 136)

Access is as above but stay to the right at the fork before Morte Lake and follow the trail around the lake. This is a more strenuous section and the 3 km loop will add about an hour to your hiking time. At the west end of Morte Lake the trail crosses Quadra Conservancy property. Please respect this area by staying on the trail.

Chinese Mountains

The access road into the Chinese Mountains is 6.7 km from the Heriot Bay store and 600 m north of Walcan Road.

The trail to the North Peak is easier, but the view from the South Peak is far more spectacular with a panorama of the Coast Range, Desolation Sound, islands, inlets, the Strait of Georgia and the Vancouver Island Mountains. Moss-covered rock ridges and weather worn stunted growth provide both peaks with a sub-alpine characteristic at only 250 to 300 m of elevation. The Chinese Mountains area has a particular reputation for ticks, in season.[i] Check carefully after a hike that you haven't gained such an unwanted friend.

(c) South and North Peak Trails (Map 4B, page 137)

From the Chinese Mountains parking area take the left-hand (southwest) trail around the base of the mountain. After about 500 m keep right, uphill, at the signed fork [1]. (The trail going down is a short connection to Morte Lake Trail). The path leading to the viewpoint cairn is well marked and, on the ridge, passes a fork that leads down the east side of South Peak, permitting a round trip. Allow two to four hours for this 2.7 km loop.

Alternatively, to reach the South Peak from its east side, take the right-hand (northwest) trail from the parking area up a fairly steep old logging road. At the signed fork [2], just where the incline eases, go left. Once on the south summit ridge this trail joins the trail coming up from the west side (above) and continues to the lookout cairn.

For the North Peak, start as for the South Peak east side (above) but keep straight on where the incline eases [2]. (Note: When reaching the North Peak rock ridge from the trail, take particular note of your surroundings. It's easy to overshoot the trail on the way back, and then get lost. A sign has been installed, but this is no substitute for good backwoods skills.)

---

i   See **Creatures Great and Small** on page 19.

West Chinese Mountain Ridge

(d) Beech's Mountain Trail (Map 4B, page 136)

A new trail goes to, though not beyond, the summit of Beech's Mountain [4]. Follow the South Chinese Mountain west side trail to a signed fork [3] where the trail leaves an old logging grade for the second time before going up earthen steps onto bedrock. This is a fairly strenuous hike, reaching around 500 m in elevation, through old-growth forest and over moss-covered rock bluffs. The constantly unfolding views of the Strait of Georgia, islands and surrounding mountains are spectacular. Allow about four hours return to the Chinese Mountains parking area.

(e) West Peak: Ridge-Edge Route (Map 4B, page 136)

Beyond (northwest of) the saddle below the summit of Beech's Mountain, a now-poorly marked route continues along the edge of the ridge towards West Chinese Mountain. West Peak has some open rock, but lacks a focal point, and consequently is not particularly interesting. However the ridge-edge scramble to it certainly is because of the old-growth forest and the constantly changing vistas of the Strait of Georgia and Vancouver Island peaks within Strathcona Provincial Park. Allow around six hours, return, from the parking area.

Caution: This rugged route is suitable only for experienced hikers. The area is accessed by some well-worn trails, but once away from them, it is minimally used at present. Flagging, where it exists, is ageing; cairns are small and infrequent and the route is growing over as little maintenance has been done recently. There are no human paths to take, and because of dog-leg changes in direction, it's easy to get off-route. If this happens, keep high on the ridge-edge and you should see cairns. It should also be remembered that travel through pockets of old-growth forest might lead to a false sense of security because the open characteristic of the forest floor can soon degenerate into impenetrable second-growth. In light of these factors, and the steep slopes and bluffs throughout, the utmost care should be exercised.

Nugedzi Lakes and Mount Seymour

(f) Nugedzi Lakes Trail (Map 4B, page 136)

This 4.25 km trail begins with a boring 45-minute grunt up an old logging road. However, hikers are well rewarded by the high, mossy and beautiful ancient forest and charming Nugedzi Lakes, especially Little Nugedzi with its bonsai-like islets.

Take Hyacinthe Bay Road for 9.1 km from the Heriot Bay store, then turn left (west) onto the old Plumper Bay Road (signposted "Nugedzi Lakes"). The parking area is 100 m up the road. The trail was developed in 1991 by the Quadra Island Recreation Society in conjunction with Fletcher Challenge (now TimberWest), and is well marked. Allow 4½ hours.

A spur trail branches at the "Lily Pond", either south [5] to a lookover (half hour return) or west to a route connecting with Plumper Bay Road and Chinese Mountains. At the time of writing, a fine beaver dam interrupts this route. The dam is worth seeing from the remains of the old boardwalk just below. Beyond Nugedzi Lake another spur trail rises to a viewpoint [6] overlooking Discovery Passage (allow 1 hour return from the bridge). At the east end of the lake-edge boardwalk at Little Nugedzi (which provides access for naturalists to study and enjoy the lake/marsh transition zone) there is a 500 m link [7] to the Mount Seymour Trail.

The alternate, and in fact preferred, access now, is to take the Mount Seymour Trail (see (g) on page 138) and the short link trail (see Map 4B) to Little Nugedzi Lake.

The cabin of Bernt Ronning, a Cape Scott settler, was shadowed by two large monkey puzzle trees. The cabin is now flattened. See page195, Ronning Garden.

The Botel Park Trail starts in the tiny North Island community of Winter Harbour. See page 194.

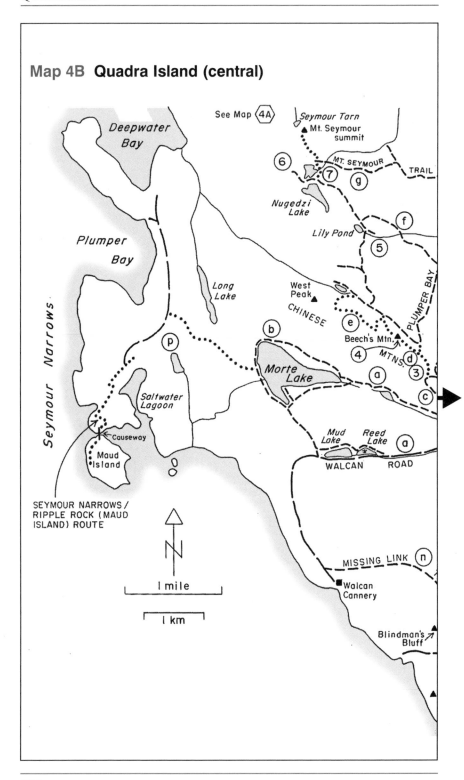

Map 4B Quadra Island (central)

Deepwater Bay

See Map 4A

Seymour Tarn
Mt. Seymour summit

6

MT. SEYMOUR

7   g   TRAIL

Nugedzi Lake

Lily Pond   f

Plumper Bay

5

Long Lake

West Peak

CHINESE

PLUMPER BAY

Seymour Narrows

p

b   e

Beech's Mtn.

4   MTNS.   d

a   3

Morte Lake   c

Saltwater Lagoon

Causeway

Maud Island

Mud Lake   Reed Lake   a

WALCAN   ROAD

SEYMOUR NARROWS /
RIPPLE ROCK (MAUD
ISLAND) ROUTE

N

1 mile

1 km

MISSING LINK   n

Walcan Cannery

Blindman's Bluff

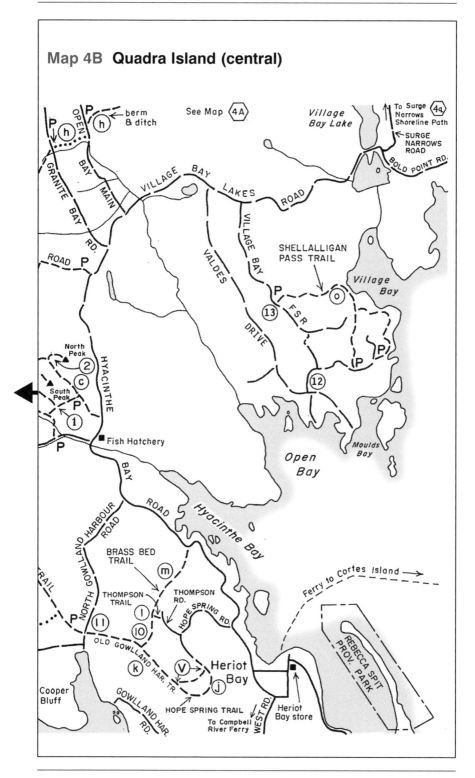

Map 4B **Quadra Island (central)**

berm & ditch

See Map 4A

OPEN BAY

P

h

h

P

Village Bay Lake

To Surge Narrows Shoreline Path 4a

←SURGE NARROWS ROAD

BOLD POINT RD.

GRANITE BAY ROAD

VILLAGE BAY MAIN RD.

VILLAGE BAY LAKES ROAD

ROAD P

VALDES DRIVE

VILLAGE BAY

SHELLALLIGAN PASS TRAIL

Village Bay

P

13

o

FSR

North Peak

2

c

HYACINTHE

South Peak

P

1

P

P

P

12

Mouids Bay

■ Fish Hatchery

Open Bay

BAY ROAD

NORTH GOWLLAND HARBOUR ROAD

Hyacinthe Bay

Ferry to Cortes Island →

BRASS BED TRAIL

m

THOMPSON TRAIL

THOMPSON RD.

HOPE SPRING RD.

TRAIL

P

11

l

10

OLD GOWLLAND HAR. TR.

k

V

j

Heriot Bay

REBECCA SPIT PROV. PARK

Cooper Bluff

GOWLLAND HAR. RD.

HOPE SPRING TRAIL

To Campbell River Ferry

WEST RD.

Heriot Bay store

(g) Mount Seymour Trail (Map 4B, page 136)

Mount Seymour (650 m) is the highest elevation on Quadra Island. Openings in the old-growth provide segmented viewscapes, though the debris from logging near the summit causes some sadness.

Follow Hyacinthe Bay Road 9.6 km from the Heriot Bay store and then take the Granite Bay Road for 2 km to Mount Seymour Trail, which is on the left (west). There is parking just beyond this point, on the right. At a fork, near the halfway mark, bear left (west). About 100 m before (east of) the short connector trail into Little Nugedzi Lake [7], a sign marks the start of the route up to the Mount Seymour summit. Follow cairns and flagging and be prepared for sharp changes in direction. When you come onto flat bedrock just below the summit, and anticipating your return, observe where the trail comes out. Below the summit a game trail goes down through old-growth to a small tarn below. Allow four to five hours for the round trip.

Northeast Quadra Island

(h) Stramberg Lake Route (Map 4A, page 131)

This route is fairly flat and can offer a tranquil, shaded walk along Stramberg Lake's eastern shore, with vistas of Mount Seymour to the west. A circuit of the lake may be made, but this is not recommended now because of the recent logging along Little Lake Main and Open Bay Main roads. We suggest going only as far as the beaver dam [8] across Stramberg Creek, and then returning the way you came. The windstorms mentioned above and open exposure over the lake may have combined to cause blowdown.

Access is near the foot of the hill on Village Bay Lakes Road, 1.2 km north of the Granite Bay turnoff. Cut left (northwest) on Open Bay Main (an active logging road) and go 1.5 km to where an earth berm and a ditch now barricade the old forest road leading towards the lake. Park along Open Bay Main but make sure you are well off the roadway. Bear left at any forks on the old forestry road, and go to the first view of the lake, where there is an access trail down to it. Go 250 m beyond this point to an old skidder road (perhaps flagged) that leads to the route along the lakeshore. Allow two to three hours, return.

A route links the Mount Seymour Trail with Stramberg Lake. It follows down and along Open Bay Creek from the trailhead on Granite Bay Road, and comes out on Open Bay Main about 300 m south of the earthen berm mentioned above. Again, there may be some blowdown.

(i) Newton Lake Trail/Small Inlet Route
(Map 4A, page 130)

This hike begins as a fairly easy forest trail, passing other lakes on the way to Newton Lake. Beyond, a more strenuous route follows an old prospectors' trail down to a promontory in Small Inlet, then links with an old portage route (it can be wet) to Waiatt Bay. With only informal consent, this route crosses private property belonging to TimberWest and Merrill & Ring Timber. Please respect this area and do not light fires or camp here.

Follow Granite Bay Road north to within 200 m of Granite Bay, and at the sign[9] turn right onto a rough road for 600 m to a fork. Stay left for this trailhead. Allow two hours, return, to Newton Lake and 4½ hours, return, to Waiatt Bay. The fork to the right is the old logging grade to Clear Lake. This is now impassable to vehicles due to a removed culvert but it makes a good hike past Two Mile Lake.

Heriot Ridge Trails

(j) Hope Spring Trail (Map 4B, page 137)

From the Heriot Bay store go 1.4 km north on Hyacinthe Bay Road to Hope Spring Road. Turn left, and go approximately 1 km to the end. The trail continues from the driveway at the very end of the road. Look for the sign. It's an easy gradient to the ridge, where a short spur leads to magnificent views towards the Coast Range to the east, and the Vancouver Island peaks in the west. Return to the Hope Spring Trail, which continues descending steeply from the ridge to the Old Gowlland Harbour Trail below.

(k) Old Gowlland Harbour[i] Trail (Map 4B, page 137)

This trail, going in a northwesterly direction, provides a valuable and attractive off-road connection between the populated south part of Quadra Island and the mid-island recreation features at Morte Lake / Chinese Mountains / Nugedzi Lakes, and of course, the historical Seymour Narrows / Ripple Rock area.

The trail passes some magnificent 300-year-old Douglas-fir. At a sign-posted fork [10], after the third bridge beyond Hope Spring Trail, you can continue north, for about an hour, on the Old Gowlland Harbour Trail which emerges on North Gowlland Harbour Road (diagonally across from the start of the Missing Link Trail [11].)

---

i **Gowlland Harbour** was named after John Thomas Gowlland, second master of HMS *Plumper* and then *Hecate*.

(l) Thompson Trail (Map 4B, page 137)

At the fork [10] mentioned above, the Thompson and Brass Bed trails combine. They go to the right, leading up to the ridge and another fork. Here the Thompson Trail goes to the right again (south) and, with some scrambling, to a viewpoint looking north from **Heriot Ridge**.[i] Signs then point the way to Thompson Road and, by making two right turns on reaching Thompson Road, a return to the starting point is achieved. Allow up to three hours for the full loop. This trail is of moderate difficulty.

(m)The Brass Bed Trail (Map 4B, page 137)

This trails goes up and over Heriot Ridge, linking the Old Gowlland Harbour Trail with the big bend in Hyacinthe Bay Road. It parallels the cascading creek, which, in the spring, provides a wonderful symphony of sound.

Other Trails

(n) Missing Link Trail (Map 4B, page 136)

The Missing Link Trail continues from the Old Gowlland Harbour Trail [11] across North Gowlland Harbour Road, where there is parking 100 m in. Once a pleasant bush track, it is now a narrow wood lot road (where the operator is attempting to preserve the integrity of the area), but as soon as it goes out of the woodlot, it becomes an industrial logging road. Keep left at the first fork, and then at the bridge just before the lake, you can take the old road along the lakeshore. Follow this up the steep hill, crossing the new road.

Further up the hill, after a sign marking "Missing Link Trail", a side-trip to the south offers worthwhile views from prominent moss-covered rock bluffs, called Blindman's Bluff. The trail continues, crossing a floating bridge (needing repair) in a wetland. It comes out just north of the cannery onto Walcan Road, which in turn leads north, past Morte Lake and the Chinese Mountains, to Hyacinthe Bay Road. If you park in this vicinity, remember that large tractor-trailers use Walcan Road at all hours.

(o) Shellalligan Pass Trail (Map 4B, page 137)

This is one of Quadra Island's newer trails and passes through two active wood lots. It parallels a rocky shoreline with a number of attractive pocket beaches that are open to the full fetch of winds up the Strait of Georgia.

---

[i] **Heriot Bay** and Ridge were named after F.L.M. Heriot, a relative of the commander-in-chief of the Royal Navy's Pacific Station.

Wave action can be spectacular. **Caution: Avoid the forest when winds are strong. Falling branches may be fatal.**

Access is from Village Bay Lakes Road, about 4 km along Valdes Drive. Enter a logging road on the left where there's a wood lot and a trail sign[12]. Drive in here around 1.7 km to the trailhead. There is parking at the trail sign just above a small bay, which you may glimpse through the trees.

Going counter-clockwise, the Shellalligan Pass Trail goes down to this bay and then follows the shore. After leaving the shoreline, it rises steeply to a (signed) fork. The **short route** is to the left (south) and will take about two hours to loop around. It reaches about 60 m in elevation. The **longer route** (which climbs as high as 100 m) goes to the right and descends again, passing two more beaches before turning inland to the Village Bay Forest Service Road (FSR)[13] and then back to the logging road on which you entered. Allow about four hours to complete a loop on this moderately difficult trail.

The trail can also be reached from the Village Bay FSR, where there are parking spots and directional signs 2.3 km south of Village Bay Lakes Road, at the point[13] where the FSR meets the inland leg of the longer route (see above).

The Maelstrom Trails

(p) Seymour Narrows / Ripple Rock (Maud Island) Route (Map 4B, page 136)

The trail/route to Seymour Narrows[i] and Ripple Rock at Maud Island starts about 100 m west of the outflow creek at Morte Lake. It currently follows an old cat track to the west, descending gradually to a logging road between Saltwater Lagoon and Plumper Bay. At the time of writing (2002), this is an attractive approach to Seymour Narrows. However, imminent road-building and active logging may drastically alter the first part of this route, and will likely change the initial access. Enquire locally at the time you make your hiking plans.

Turn left (south) on this logging road. Go about 300 m beyond a rock pit, to a sign for the trail (possibly removed) just before a "Private Property" notice. The trail is on the right (west) and goes a short distance through the clearcut into the woods. Maintain, and even gain, elevation to some rock bluffs overlooking Saltwater Lagoon and Maud Island. This route is well flagged, but remember that on occasion flagging has been removed. The

---

i   **Seymour Narrows** were named after Rear-Admiral Sir George Francis Seymour, commander of the Pacific Station 1844-1848.

trail descends steeply from these bluffs to where there is a junction with two signs. By going left (east), a short but pleasant side trip to Saltwater Lagoon is possible. This is a favourite place for wildlife.

By continuing to the right (southwest) at this fork, the trail to Seymour Narrows skirts above a small bay and then follows an old construction road to a rock causeway leading across to Maud Island. It's interesting to watch water going through the rockfill when the tide is higher on one side than the other. Once on Maud Island, an incline leads up, at one point sharply, passing more of the Ripple Rock tunneling activities, to an excellent viewpoint overlooking Seymour Narrows. See page 153 for the history of Ripple Rock.

The massive whirlpools and current movement, which at full flood combine in a gentle roar, can be awe-inspiring to watch. Currents here can attain speeds of 16 knots. It is worth checking the time of maximum flow beforehand. If at all possible, go when the water is running at its fastest. Consult the **Canadian Tide and Current Tables, Vol. 6,** published by the Canadian Hydrographic Service. This is a fairly long and strenuous hike so allow at least five or six hours round-trip from Morte Lake, plus whirlpool-gazing time.

(q) Surge Narrows Shoreline Path
(Map 4B, page 137; see also Map 5, page 144)

This is a moderate hike along the shoreline from the end of the road to Surge Narrows in the Settler's Group Provincial Marine Park. The route is an interesting woods walk and passes beaches, goes over bluffs, and follows ledges above tidal rapids. It offers a mixture of forest and shoreline, with views of islets, whirlpools and wildlife. As at Seymour Narrows, it's worth checking and arranging to be there at maximum flood. Allow three to four hours, return, plus a bit.

Access is from the Heriot Bay store. Take Hyacinthe Bay Road to Village Bay Lakes Road. After crossing the Village Bay Lake bridge, bear left (north) onto Surge Narrows Road and go past Mine Lake. It's 6.2 km from the bridge to the end of the road. Park above the steep incline to the beach. **Do not drive down to the water unless you have a high-slung four-wheel-drive vehicle.**

The route starts from the lower parking area, although at the time of writing (2002) there was no sign or flagging here to mark it. Cross the creek to a small saddle, just on the other (north) side. From here much of the route is a well-trodden path – and there is flagging! In a few places where the route is indistinct, an interpretation of the lie of the land, or a glimpse of distant tape, soon comes to the rescue.

The path leads to three main points of interest overlooking Canoe Pass and Surge Narrows. The first of these, which offers the best view of the tidal rapids and islets, is marked with a temporary sign in a large open draw with moss-covered boulders, reached after descending a loose-earth side-hill. At times of maximum flood, the difference in water level between the Surge Narrows and the Hoskyn Channel sides can easily be seen from here.

Another point of interest is from the bay just to the north. The path continues over a rise, along a ledge above the rapids where there is a 3 m scramble. At the time of writing (2002), a fixed rope at this point is helpful. The third place of interest is a small islet at the south end of Surge Narrows proper. It's along the shore and around the corner from the north end of this bay and is accessible at low tide. It presents quite a different view of the islands and Beazley Passage. For current and tidal information, refer to the *Canadian Tide and Current Tables, Vol. 6*, published by the Canadian Hydrographic Service.

Quadra Island material contributed by Noel Lax

NOTES:

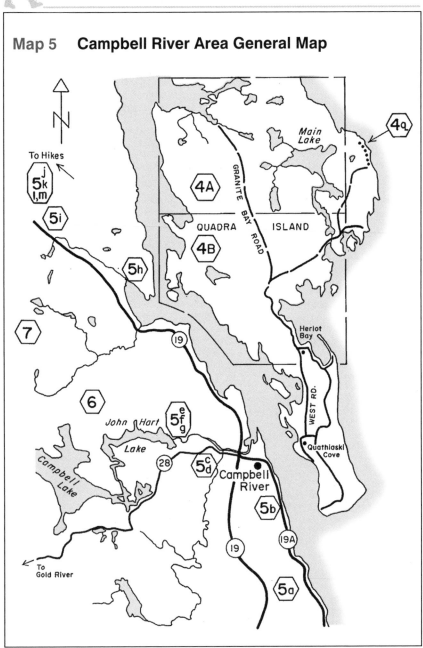

Map 5 Campbell River Area General Map

5A. Campbell River Area

The Campbell River Search and Rescue Society produces their *Logging and Highway Road Map*, a recreation and logging road guide of the Campbell River[i] region, showing much useful information. This map covers the area north of Strathcona Provincial Park as far as Sayward, and is available at most sporting goods stores. (See *Map Sources* on page 21.) Weyerhaeuser's *Recreation and Logging Road Guide to TFL 39* is also useful. (See *Logging Companies* on page 24.) *Nature Campbell River*, by Christine Scott, describes 37 trails in the Campbell River area.

All over Canada, work proceeds on the **National Hiking Trail** (not to be confused with the Trans Canada Trail) that will stretch coast to coast across the country. In a few regions this single-use (hiking only) corridor will follow the same route as the Trans Canada Trail (which is multi-use); in others it will be a viable hiking alternative. Planning for a potential route between Nanaimo and Campbell River continues. For current information contact www.nationaltrail.ca

(a) Willow Creek Nature Trust Trails

(Map 5(a), page 146)

Located at the south end of Campbell River, these trails are accessed from the Highway 19A via Erickson Road, and also from Dahl, Martin, Willow Creek or Twillingate roads. You can also come in from the Inland Island Highway (Highway 19) via the Jubilee Parkway and South Dogwood Street.

The Willow Creek trails provide a beautiful forest and wetland walk along Willow Creek, a salmon enhancement stream and valuable fish habitat. From a parking lot at Erickson Road the trail drops downhill to the stream. Turn east (left) and follow the stream bank to an extension of Martin Road where you cross the stream on a footbridge and return down the other bank.

There are many interesting branch trails. Along these paths (particularly those near Willow Creek) are great opportunities for bird watching. Look for a variety of woodpeckers, including the red-breasted sapsucker. Many hikers time their visits for viewing seasonal wildflowers and plantlife. Improvements include benches, wooden boardwalks and footbridges. Trails can be very wet and muddy in the winter and spring. Leash all pets.

The land comprising Willow Creek Nature Trails (34.2 ha) is held by BC Nature Trust, with stewardship, since the spring of 1995, by the Willow Creek Watershed Society.

i   Dr. Samuel **Campbell** was assistant surgeon on HM survey ship *Plumper*, 1857-61.

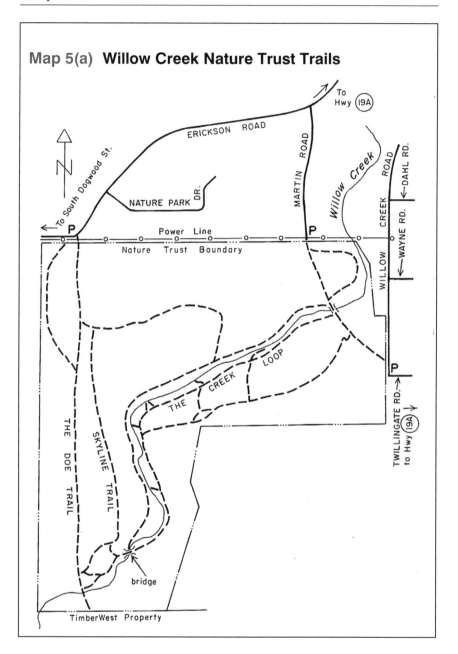

Map 5(a) Willow Creek Nature Trust Trails

(b) Beaver Lodge Lands Trails (Map 5(b), page 147)

This large forestland (415 ha) on the southwest side of Campbell River, and adjacent to new subdivisions, is being developed by the BCFS for recreation. At present, trails are multiple-use and accommodate hikers, horses, walkers, runners and mountain bikers. These trails vary in skill level and character, but are mostly "easy" for hikers.

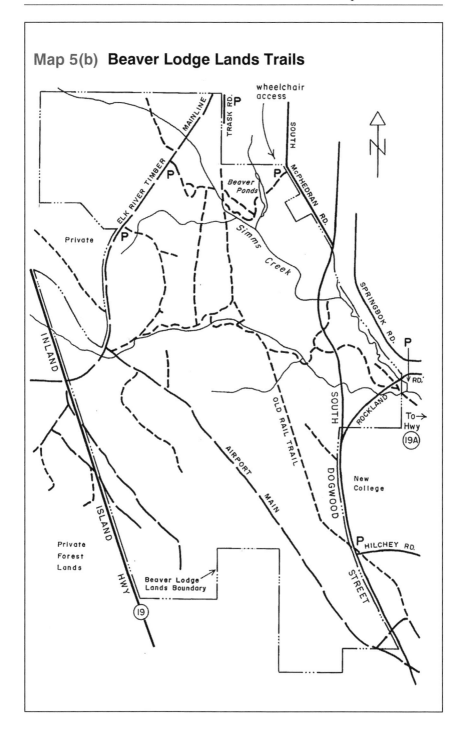

Map 5(b) **Beaver Lodge Lands Trails**

The Beaver Lodge Lands Trails are accessed from Hilchey Road, Rockland Road, South McPhedran Road (with wheelchair access), South Dogwood Street, Trask Road and the Elk River Timber (ERT) Mainline.

The trail along **Simms Creek** has long been popular, and there are a number of ways to incorporate it into a circular tour from any of the parking areas. The Simms Creek Trail is an even-grade path, providing an easy walk suitable for most users. The trail system provides an interesting diversity of flora and fauna, including swamp life.

This region is habitat for a variety of wildflowers, birds, and amphibians, even bears and bats. In 1998, a butterfly corridor project, spearheaded by the Vancouver Island Butterfly Enthusiasts and sponsored initially by the BCFS and the Canada Trust Friends of the Environment Fund, resulted in a butterfly garden being planted near Hilchey Road.

Improvements include footbridges and signposts at the trailheads. A kilometre-long fine gravel wheelchair trail can be accessed off South McPhedran Road. Area trails are generally wet and muddy in winter and early spring, though their improved, well-packed surfaces have aided drainage. It takes about two hours to complete a loop walk.

(c) Quinsam River Nature Trail (Map 5(c/d), page 149)

The trailhead is under the Quinsam River Bridge, on Highway 28, approximately 1.6 km west of the junction of highways 19, 19A and 28, near the Campbell River bridge. This trail follows the Quinsam River[i] for 3.3 km to the salmon hatchery. A round trip takes about two hours. It is in good condition and provides an easy walk through a beautiful area. During the spawning season, salmon can be seen returning up the river. The BC Parks Quinsam River Campsite (within Elk Falls Provincial Park and along Highway 28) provides drinking water and toilet facilities. The Quinsam River Nature Trail connects with the Canyon View Trail, near the Quinsam River bridge. From here you can follow the south bank of the Campbell River for 1.2 km to the BC Hydro power station. See 5(e) on page 150.

For information on the Quinsam Salmon Hatchery contact (250) 287-9564.

(d) Beaver Pond Trail (Map 5(c/d), page 149)

The Beaver Pond Trail is a short (approximately 1 km) connecting link between the Quinsam River Nature Trail and the Canyon View Trail.

---

i *Quinsam* means "resting place" in the language of the Comox people.

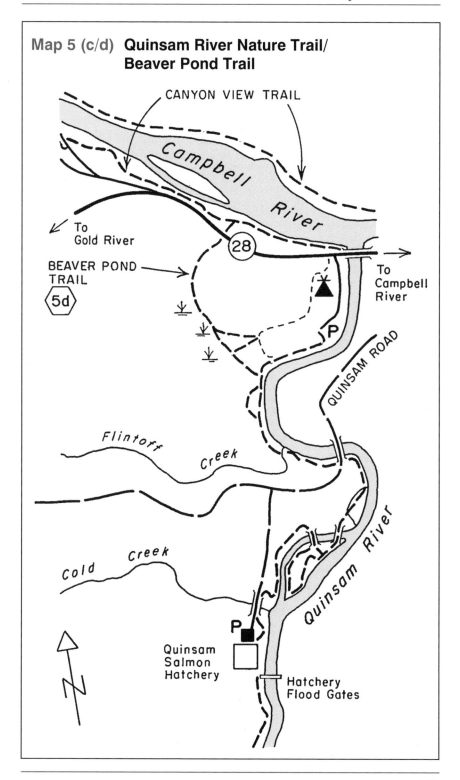

Map 5 (c/d) **Quinsam River Nature Trail/ Beaver Pond Trail**

CANYON VIEW TRAIL

Campbell River

To Gold River

BEAVER POND TRAIL

5d

28

To Campbell River

QUINSAM ROAD

Flintoff Creek

Cold Creek

Quinsam River

P

P

Quinsam Salmon Hatchery

Hatchery Flood Gates

N

(e) Canyon View Trail (Map 5(e), page 151)

Warning: Water levels in the Campbell River fluctuate due to periodic water release from the John Hart Dam. Loud warning sirens will sound to indicate there is a danger of suddenly rising water. Evacuate the riverbank immediately when you hear the sirens.

From the junction of Highways 19, 19A and 28, near the Campbell River bridge, drive 2.3 km west towards Gold River on Highway 28. At the bottom of the big hill swing right, to BC Hydro's John Hart Generating Station, and follow the signs to the visitor parking area. Keep out of signposted restricted-access areas. There are toilets, a picnic day-use area and several viewing platforms.

The Canyon View Trail was built in 1991 with the support of BC Parks, BC Hydro, Campbell River Lions Club, Fletcher Challenge (now TimberWest), Ministry of Transportation and Highways, Pacific Coast Energy and the community of Campbell River.

No camping or fires are allowed. Obey all warning signs. Leash all pets. Stay on designated trails to help minimize environmental damage. Wear sturdy footwear. Use caution and watch for vehicles when hiking across the TimberWest logging-road bridge and the Quinsam River bridge, on Highway 28. The trail is open between 8 am and dusk.

On the Canyon View Trail you can complete a 6 km, two-hour loop along both sides of the Campbell River. There are some steep steps and hills. The river is crossed twice: once via a footbridge in the canyon, and again via the TimberWest logging road bridge, farther downstream. A highlight is the canyon footbridge, 24.4 m long, that hides the natural gas pipeline underneath. The 2.5 km Millennium Trail links Canyon View Trail with trails in Elk Falls Provincial Park and begins near the canyon footbridge. See Map 5(g) on page 152.

The Campbell River was officially designated a BC Heritage River in March 2000. In the spring of 2002, the Outdoor Recreation Council of BC named the Campbell and the Quinsam rivers to a list of BC's second-most-endangered steelhead rivers.

(f) Millennium Trail (Map 5(e), page 151; Map 5(g), page 152)

The Millennium Trail, completed in 2001, runs 2.5 km along the south side of the Campbell River and connects the Canyon View Trail with the Elk Falls viewpoint. The steeper sections are closer to the John Hart Generating Station where there are several long series of steps. Stay away from the canyon's sheer cliffs.

Map 5(e) Canyon View Trail

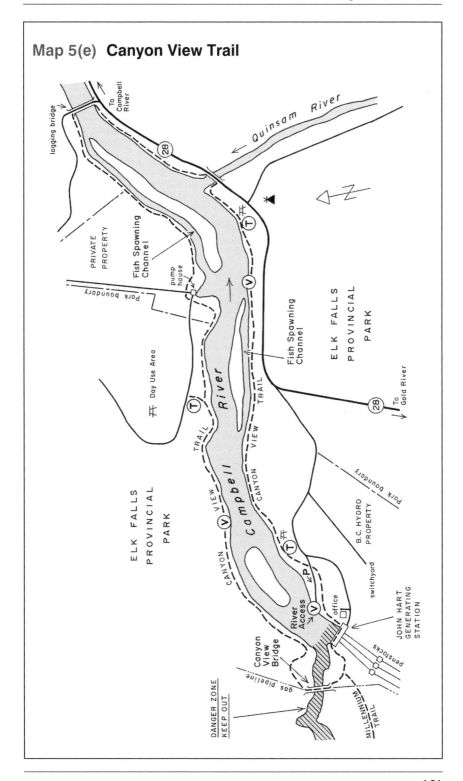

(g) Elk Falls Provincial Park Trails (Map 5(g), below)

This series of trails is accessible at **Elk Falls Provincial Park (1087 ha)**. The access road is located along Highway 28, about 6.5 km west of its junction with Highway 19 and Highway 19A, near Campbell River. Turn off the highway at the top of "General Hill" onto Brewster Lake Road, cross a wooden bridge (the road to the left provides a view of the dam) to a fork in the road. The road to the right goes to a parking lot that overlooks the falls; the road on the left features groves of big timber. The main trail is approximately 2 km long, is quite steep in some sections, and can be slippery during rainy periods. It takes about 45 minutes for a round trip.

The trail follows the Campbell River from Moose Falls to Elk Falls, providing a beautiful walk through an area with gigantic Douglas-fir and cedar trees, some of which are 800 years old, and views of the numerous pools along the river course. The lookout provides a scenic view of Elk Falls, where the water tumbles some 25 m to the bottom and into Elk Falls canyon. The Millennium Trail, opened in 2001, links this area with the Canyon View Trail. See also 5(f) on page 150.

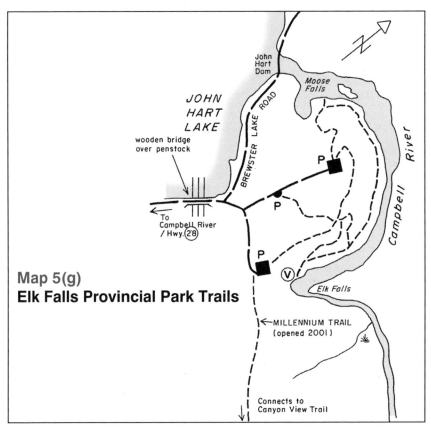

**Map 5(g)
Elk Falls Provincial Park Trails**

5B. Campbell River / Sayward Area

(h) Ripple Rock Trail (Map 5(h), page 154)

The Ripple Rock Trail is a 1½ to 2 hour hike (one way) leading to the Seymour Narrows lookout and views across to Quadra and Maud islands. The marked trailhead is 17 km north of the Campbell River bridge, near the junction of Highways 19, 19A and 28. The signposted parking area is on the east side of Highway 19.

The trail is 4 km long, with an easy-to-moderate grade to **Menzies Bay**[i] and a steep section to Wilfred Point. It passes through areas that were logged about 70 years ago and now have Douglas-fir, red alder, broadleaf maple and western hemlock. On the east side of Menzies Creek the trail passes through two small patches of old-growth with 300-year-old Sitka spruce and Douglas-fir. There are good viewpoints along the trail and a nice sandy beach at Nymphe Cove. The trail was constructed in 1983 through a grant sponsored by the Campbell River Rotary Club.

Midway between the lookout and Maud Island is the site of the infamous Ripple Rock, two menacing rock pinnacles whose summits used to provide only a few metres clearance at low tide. This notorious marine hazard caused damage to dozens of ships and claimed 114 lives, resulting in a project to destroy Ripple Rock by blowing it to pieces. In 1958, the largest man-made, non-nuclear explosion in history reduced the rock by 370,000 tonnes to create a clearance of 13 m. In 1984, a cruise ship was holed off Maud Island and, although it limped to Duncan Bay, it sank at the dock.

i   Archibald **Menzies** (1754-1842) was a surgeon on Captain Vancouver's *Discovery*, but he was also a botanist, so we find his name appended to many plant names, notably the *Arbutus menziesii*.

153

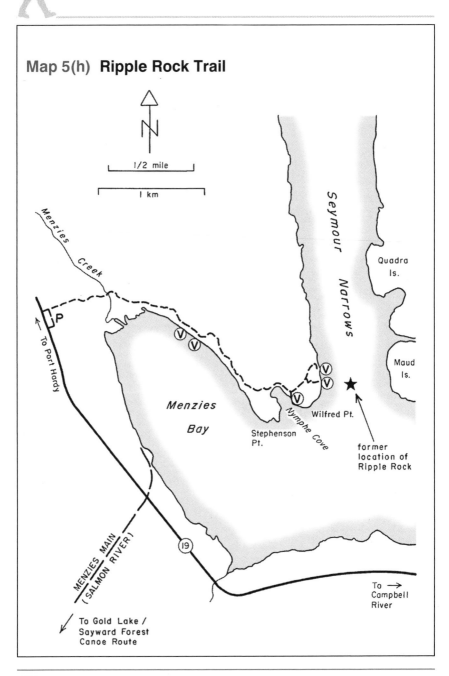

Map 5(h) Ripple Rock Trail

(i) Menzies Mountain Trail (Map 5(i))

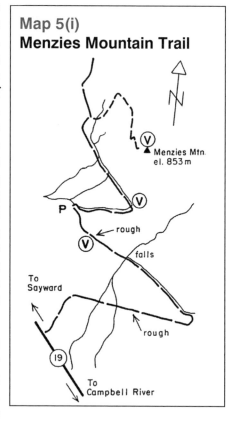

Map 5(i)
Menzies Mountain Trail

Access to Menzies Mountain is off Highway 19, just over 24 km from the junction of Highway 19, Highway 19A and Highway 28 in Campbell River. The turnoff is on the east side of Highway 19. If there is active logging in the area, the road can be driven as far as the second lookout, although caution should be taken during work hours and right-of-way given to logging trucks. This is a narrow gravel road with not many pullouts and there are numerous, confusing side roads. The upper stretches are rough and require a high-slung four-wheel-drive vehicle. The parking area (if you can reach it) has room for four or five vehicles.

The strenuous 3 km Menzies Mountain Trail is somewhat rocky and has some steep sections. It provides spectacular views in all directions, especially of the Sayward Forest and the mountains of Vancouver Island. Allow at least two hours, return, from the indicated parking area, more if bad road conditions require you to park lower down and trudge up the logging road.

(j) McNair Lake Trail

The McNair Lake Trail, near the northwest end of Roberts Lake, winds 1.8 km west along a logging road to McNair Lake. This is a popular mountain-biking area. Watch for the trailhead on the left (west) side of Highway 19, about 32.5 km north of the Highway 19, Highway 19A and Highway 28 junction, near the Campbell River bridge.

(k) Salmon Lookout Trail

The Salmon Lookout Trail is approximately 50.5 km north of the Highway 19, Highway 19A and Highway 28 junction in Campbell River. The trail climbs sharply for 3 km to an old forestry lookout and spectacular vista of the Salmon River Valley. Allow two hours for the return trip.

(l) Dalrymple Creek Trail

Just 9 km east of the Sayward Junction or around 55.5 km north of the Highway 19, Highway 19A and Highway 28 junction in Campbell River is the Dalrymple Creek Recreation Trail. From the small parking area on the north side of Highway 19, visitors can enjoy an easy 0.5 km forest walk through private Weyerhaeuser forestlands.

(m) Bill's Trail (Mount H'Kusam)

Accessed from the corner of Sabre Road, near Sayward, Bill's Trail climbs up Mount H'Kusam to an elevation of 1670 m. There are plenty of breath-taking vistas so don't forget your camera. The highlight is an expansive view over Salmon Bay and the Salmon River estuary. This is a steep climb in a wilderness environment so carry adequate mountain hiking gear. Some sections are overgrown. A round trip takes about six hours.

Improving the trail is a labour of love for Bill West-Sells and his helpers. Work continues on trail clearing and maintenance. Contact (250) 282-3818 for more information or to volunteer to help. A trail map is available at the White River Court tourist information centre, near the Sayward Junction.

6. Snowden Demonstration Forest
(Map 6, page 160)

The Snowden Demonstration Forest was designed to raise public awareness about Integrated Resource Management in provincial forests. In this "active" forest, silvicultural systems are integrated with other forest interests including recreation. An extensive system of trails in this area, while perhaps not for the purist or those who prefer alpine hiking, provides a variety of interpretive and recreational forest-based opportunities suitable for all ages. Mountain bikes are allowed on the trails.

This area is just outside Campbell River. From the junction of Highways 19, 19A and 28, near the Campbell River bridge, follow Highway 28 about 6.5 km toward Gold River. At the top of the big hill ("General Hill") take the right turn onto Brewster Lake Road, heading to Elk Falls Provincial Park. At the sign for Loveland Bay stay left and cross the John Hart Dam. Follow the directional signs from there.

Interpretive Trails:
Three hiking trails are located on Snowden Road:

- **Old Forest Trail**: 325 m long, a 15-minute walk through an old-growth forest.

- **Ecosystem Trail**: 800 m, shows examples of forest ecology.

- **Silviculture Trail**: 1.1 km. The complete forest management cycle is examined, from site preparation to planting, tending and harvesting.

Check with the BCFS Campbell River District office about the availability of area brochures. The BCFS originally constructed 40 km of trails here. Local mountain bike clubs have built over 60 km of routes. A biker's route map is available at several Campbell River bike stores.

Recreational Trails:
Numerous trails provide opportunities for hiking, cycling, running and mushroom picking.

Frog Lake Trail System
(1) **Old Rail Trail**: 4.2 km along a historical rail grade. The trailhead is located north of Elmer Lake on the Frog Lake Road.

(2) **Lookout Loop**: 3.2 km. The loop starts from the Frog Lake Road, climbing up and over rocky outcrops, then down through forest and wetland areas. It joins up with the Old Rail Trail.

(3) **Enchanted Forest**: 4.3 km through lush forest and along rough gravel roads. Cyclists are recommended to ride this loop in a clockwise direction.

(4) **Riley Lake Connector**: 1.9 km of forest trail and old rail grade that connects Enchanted Forest and Lost Lake Trails.

(5) **Headbanger Hookup**: This route is principally for cyclists.

Lost Lake Trail System

(6) **Lost Lake Trail**: 5.5 km loop with picnic tables at the south end of the lake. Short hike to rocky viewpoint.

(7) **Mudhoney Pass**: Principally for cyclists.

(8) **The Lost Frog**: 8.2 km of almost-continuous rail grade, with a few rougher connections. Access is via the north end of Devlin Road or Frog Lake Road.

(9) **Frog Lake Road**: 5.7 km, an optional link between Frog Lake and Lost Lake trail systems.

Exploring a trail in the Snowden Demonstration Forest

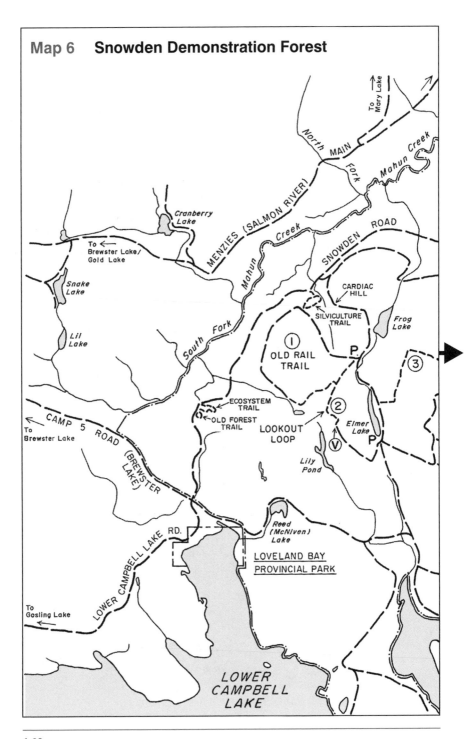

Map 6   Snowden Demonstration Forest

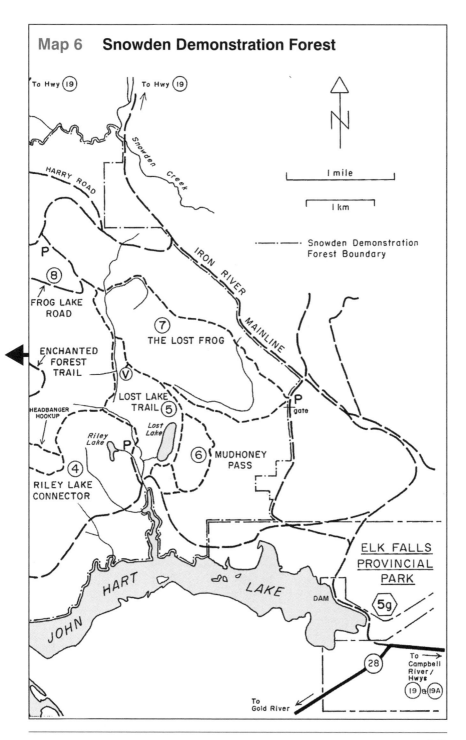

Map 6   Snowden Demonstration Forest

To Hwy (19)
To Hwy (19)

N

| 1 mile |

| 1 km |

——·—— Snowden Demonstration Forest Boundary

Snowden Creek

HARRY ROAD

IRON RIVER MAINLINE

P

(8)
FROG LAKE ROAD

(7)
THE LOST FROG

ENCHANTED FOREST TRAIL

(V)

LOST LAKE TRAIL (5)

P
gate

HEADBANGER HOOKUP

Riley Lake
Lost Lake

P

(6) MUDHONEY PASS

(4)
RILEY LAKE CONNECTOR

ELK FALLS PROVINCIAL PARK

JOHN HART LAKE

DAM

(5g)

(28)

To
Campbell River/ Hwys
(19) & (19A)

To
Gold River

7. Sayward Forest

(Map 7, page 164)

The Sayward Forest was named after William Parsons Sayward, a pioneer logger and sawmill operator. The terrain is an undulating area largely covered with immature and some maturing second-growth timber. There are numerous lakes and creeks. In 1938 a large forest fire burned much of the area. The forest was subsequently replanted and today this is the most intensively managed forest in BC. The public is invited to participate with the Sayward Forest Landscape Unit.

The BCFS has developed rustic recreation sites throughout the area in conjunction with a continuous canoe and portage route. The Sayward Forest Canoe Route is approximately 40 km in length and includes about 7 km of portages, recently upgraded and widened. Most of these lake links accommodate canoes that are portaged on wheels. A circuit of this eleven-lake system takes most canoeists about three to four days.

The Sayward Forest Canoe Route is best accessed at Morton Lake Provincial Park. From the junction of Highways 19, 19A and 28, near the Campbell River bridge, keep north on Highway 19. Drive 14.5 km to Weyerhaeuser's Menzies Bay (Salmon River) Mainline. Swing west on the mainline and continue 9.5 km west to the park access road. From here it's about 6.5 km to Morton Lake.

Check with Weyerhaeuser's North Islands Timberlands Division for updates on truck hauling, road conditions and access restrictions. (See *Logging Companies* on page 24.) Contact the BCFS Campbell River District office about the availability of a canoe route brochure giving route details and safety precautions. There are no plans to reprint the pamphlet when current supplies run out.

A trail to Andrew Lake begins near Morton Lake Provincial Park, in the Sayward Forest.

Gray Lake is part of the Sayward Forest Canoe Route.

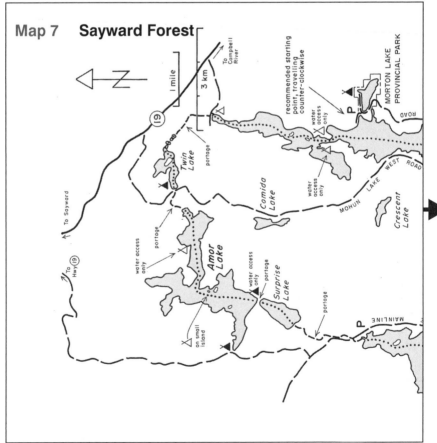

Map 7 Sayward Forest

1 mile

3 km

To Campbell River

(19)

To Sayward

To Hwy (19)

Twin Lake

portage

Comida Lake

Amor Lake

portage

water access only

on small island

Surprise Lake

portage

water access only

recommended starting point, travelling counter-clockwise

water access only

water access only

MORTON LAKE PROVINCIAL PARK

P

ROAD

MOHUN LAKE WEST ROAD

Crescent Lake

portage

MAINLINE

P

Fry Lake, with its stands of dead snags, is part of the Sayward Forest Canoe Route.

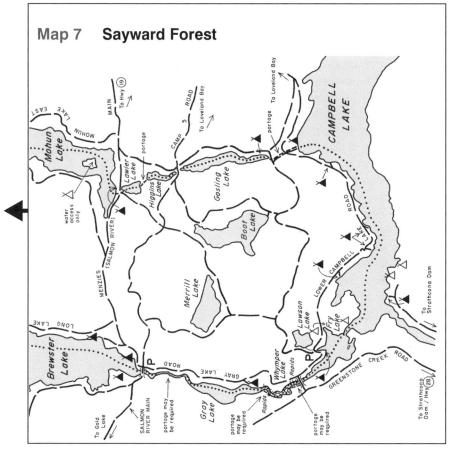

Map 7   **Sayward Forest**

8. Gold River Area

White Ridge Provincial Park (1343 ha), named for its white limestone (part of the karst[i] topography that exists here), is located between Strathcona Provincial Park's northwest boundary and Highway 28. Roughly about 4 km east of Gold River, this forested ridge is prime elk and deer habitat. There are no facilities or services and the area is not regularly patrolled.

(a) Victoria Peak Route

Drive 3 km north from Gold River, cross the Gold River bridge to a sign-posted T-junction. Swing right onto Nimpkish Road heading toward Woss. (A left goes to the Upana Caves and Tahsis.) Just over 8.5 km north from the Gold River bridge, at a fork, cut right (east) onto West Main. Follow up the Gold River Valley about 14 km to a triangle intersection. Keep left here. (If you go right, you will cross the bridge over the Gold River onto East Road, which provides access to a rugged hiking route to Gold Lake, from the west. See **Gold Lake Access** on page 63.

From here continue another 4 km (the road roughens and may require a high-slung four-wheel-drive vehicle) and you will see Twaddle Lake through the trees on your right. About one kilometre past the lake, near the White/Gold Pass, **Victoria Peak (2163 m)** will appear in the distance. Turn right onto W-79, the last branch road before the road ends. From here you will need a four-wheel-drive vehicle as the road through the big, open slash has been deactivated and culverts removed. Wind your way up through the slash and park where the road turns sharply right, at the edge of the forest on the most-northern point of the slash.

From the rough parking area, at the 975 m level, head almost due east and pick your way up through a steep area of logging slash to get onto the south ridge of Victoria Peak. Hike a short distance north to pick up an indistinct west-east ridge (remnant flags) and follow this 1 km east to the main divide, 3 km south of Victoria Peak. It should take about 30-45 minutes to gain the ridge. The trail through the heather is obvious (once you find it). From here, the trail follows the south ridge, which gets quite narrow at times. Head north over a bump. There is good camping (with space for two tents) at a large tarn, which is located about two hours from the parking area. Climbers who plan to go for the Victoria Peak summit usually use this campsite.

---

i   See footnote, page 186

From here you can walk along the ridge for another one or two hours before you reach the massif itself and are faced with technical climbing. The route to the summit involves some low 5th class climbing and a fair amount of exposed scrambling. Mountaineering experience is required. Finding the route can be a problem and expect to use a rope, at least in one section. It is necessary to drop east off the main south ridge and locate a bench that leads into the east-facing snow bowl below Victoria Peak's south face in order to bypass an insurmountable gap. Use crampons to cross the bowl in late season. Avoid the scree-threatened cliffs and scramble east toward the sky-line of the east ridge to the end of the cliffs on good ledges. A rock climb and scramble west leads to the summit. Many people day-hike to the south ridge, climb up close to Victoria Peak and then head back down. Allow four to five hours for a return hike.

Contact Western Forest Products in Gold River for updates on road conditions and access restrictions. Use their *Visitors Guide to Logging Roads and Recreation Areas (Nootka Region)* (see *Logging Companies* on page 24.)

Special thanks to **Chris Barner**, **Sandy Briggs** and **Kent Krauza** for their reports.

(b) Upana Caves (Map 8(b), page 168)

The Upana Caves are located 17 km northwest of Gold River on the Head Bay Forest Road (to Tahsis). Driving time from Gold River is 25 minutes. The trail is mostly a surface trail of about 400 m through an immature forest (replanted) setting. Once at Upana Caves you have the added opportunity to observe, and explore, a natural cave system. Pick up a self-guided tour brochure from the BCFS Campbell River District office or at a travel infocentre.

These notes are taken from the Upana Caves brochure:

The first systematic exploration and mapping of these caves was undertaken in 1975 by recreational cavers. Cavers named the cave system after the Upana River, which flows through one of the caves. The cave interiors remain in a relatively wild, undeveloped state.

The Upana Caves are comprised of several individual caves ranging in size from single rooms to branching passages of varying length. There are 15 known entrances within the system, and the combined length of cave passages is approximately 450 m.

To safely explore the caves you should carry a reliable flashlight or head-lamp. A good light will help you to see the cave features and to watch your footing on uneven floors. The Upana Caves are a year-round experience. No matter what the weather is outside, the temperature inside the caves averages a chilly 7° Celsius, so bring a sweater or jacket.

It is very important that visitors be careful not to disturb the cave environment. Keep to the established trails and underground routes, do not touch delicate cave formations, and refrain from smoking and lighting fires.

Editor's note: A second source of light (another flashlight or candles and matches) is a good safety factor.

The Tahsis Lions Club's annual "Great Walk" follows the Head Bay FSR for 63.5 km, all the way from Gold River to Tahsis. To learn more about this fund-raising trek, touted as North America's toughest pledge walk, contact the Tahsis Lions Club, PO Box 430, Tahsis, BC V0P 1X0.

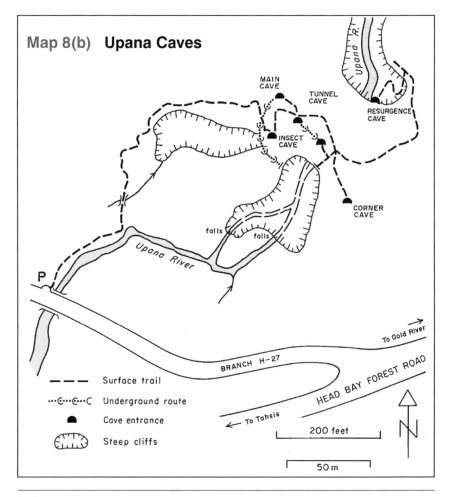

Map 8(b)   Upana Caves

9. The Nootka Trail (Nootka Island)
(Map 9A, page 174 / Map 9B, page 176)

The Nootka Trail is a remote, unpatrolled wilderness destination. Hikers must be experienced with coastal travel and geared for extreme adverse weather conditions.

The Nootka Trail doesn't exist — at least, not officially. However, this rugged 35 km route along Nootka Island's west coast has been travelled for thousands of years. The village of Yuquot is at least 4300 years old. It was here, in 1778, that the Nu-chah-nulth people greeted Captain Cook and his crew, the first Europeans on the west coast.

The normal start for hikers is at the trail's north end. Floatplanes can land in Louie Bay Lagoon, where visitors disembark, usually into waist-deep water. (Shorts and sandals are recommended.) A rugged trail heads south through an old-growth forest to Third Beach. This is the roughest part of the hike. At beautiful Third Beach you'll discover an expansive 1 km sandy beach where there is camping and water. Hiking time from Louie Bay Lagoon to Third Beach is 45 minutes to one hour.

You can day-hike northwest from Third Beach to a saltwater narrows at Louie Bay's south end. This waterway is passable only at tides of 1.8 m or less. Tidal information is crucial here and all along the Nootka Trail. You don't want to get trapped by high tides. Consult the ***Canadian Tide and Current Tables, Vol. 6.***

From the narrows, head north along the mudflats to Tongue Point. Here you'll find the remains of a hull from a wrecked ship, moved here as part of an unsuccessful salvage operation. The Greek ship *Tries Ierarchi* smashed into the rocks in late 1969, southeast of Ferrer Point.

With time and tides in your favour, you can consider following a somewhat overgrown road from Tongue Point to Northwest Cone where there are the ruins of an early radar installation. (Estimated one-way hiking times: Third Beach to the narrows, one hour; the narrows to Tongue Point, one hour; Tongue Point to **Northwest Cone**[i], one hour.)

From Third Beach, the Nootka Trail cuts inland to avoid a tricky headland about 1 km to the southeast. Watch for floats and buoys hanging in the trees at the start of the bypass route. The beach route is passable only on an extreme low tide. South of the headland, hike along the tidal shelf to Skuna Bay, where you'll find good camping and water.

---

i   **cone:** This geographic term refers to a small, pointed hill or mountain.

Another tricky beach passage is just before Calvin Creek. Calvin Creek empties Crawfish and Ewart lakes. Calvin Falls, 6 m high, is a trail highlight. There is good camping and water here. Estimated hiking time from Third Beach to Calvin Falls is 4 or 5 hours.

The beach is the usual route from Calvin Falls to Beano Creek. South of the falls the trail crosses Bajo Creek, an unreliable water source due to its brackish nature. Bajo Point is a First Nations Reserve and an ancient village site, once known as E'as. Respect this private land. From the point you can watch for whales and sea otters. The latter were successfully re-introduced to the area, over 30 years ago. (By the mid-1800s, the indigenous otters had been depleted by early fur trading.) At Beano Creek there is camping and water. The ancient whaling village of Tsarksis was located nearby. The tricky crossing at Beano Creek is easiest at low tide. Approximate hiking time from Calvin Falls to Beano Creek is 3 to 4 hours.

To avoid impassable headlands and surge channels, hikers are forced onto the inland trail, just north of Callicum Creek. There is camping and water on the beach near the creekmouth. Fill up your water here, as this is the last reliable source until you reach a small beach near Yuquot. The inland trail runs along the cliffs and is somewhat exposed. Pocket beaches can be accessed via challenging side trails. Drop your packs at the side of the main trail and take the short (a 10-minute walk) path to Maquinna Point and a spectacular seascape. Under a kilometre south of Maquinna Point, a shore access route drops down to a beach with three sea caves.

There is good swimming at the wide narrows where a tidal saltwater river flows in and out of a lagoon (Tsa'tsil). It's a formidable torrent at times, but traverseable and not very deep at low tide. You can camp here (the south side is best) but there is no water. The next spot for camping and water is a pocket beach to the south. Allow at least 8 or 9 hours hiking time between Beano Creek and the tidal lagoon. Many hikers make this a two-day stretch.

The trail between the tidal lagoon and Yuquot (part of **Yatz-mahs Trails**) is maintained by the Mowachaht/Muchalat Band, the Ministry of Forests, and Western Forest Products (WFP). Other trails lead through old-growth trees to an unnamed lake and Jewitt (Aa-aak-quaksius) Lake. Hiking time from the lagoon to Yuquot is around 1.5 hours.

The Nootka Trail terminates at Yuquot and Friendly Cove. There is a $5.00 fee to cross the First Nations land and visit the historical museum (a former church). Only one family remains at Yuquot. The other Mowachaht Band members moved to the Gold River area in 1968. You can camp near Yuquot or rent one of six small cabins. For more information contact:

Mowachaht/Muchalaht First Nation Band Office, Box 459, Gold River, BC V0P 1G0 (250) 283-2335; 1-800-238-2933 (toll-free); (250) 283-2335 (fax); e-mail: info@yuquot.ca.

The dock at Yuquot accommodates floatplanes, the *MV Uchuck III* out of Gold River, and a water taxi service. The nearby Friendly Cove lighthouse still has a lightkeeper. **Santa Gertrudis-Boca Del Infierno Provincial Marine Park (440 ha)** protects a coastal marine environment and an old-growth forest, north of Friendly Cove. The park can only be accessed by water. The bay is a sheltered anchorage for paddlers and boaters.

The Nootka Trail is mostly on Crown Land and falls within a Special Management Zone, a category that recognizes the region's intrinsic wilderness and historical importance, yet does not save the area from future development. The old-growth trail from Louie Bay Lagoon to Third Beach is not protected. The Land Use Plan's buffer zone is only 200 m in width, while, in places, the trail extends inland much farther than that. Future development and leasing for recreation and rural purposes could occur on several tracts of private land. That possibility, and area logging, could impact the wilderness experience.

Even five years ago, not many people knew of the Nootka Trail. That is slowly changing. Last year about 400 hikers visited the area and in 2002, the number was expected to increase to 700. The opportunity to save all of the Nootka Trail for future generations may be fleeting. Contact your MLA and voice your opinion. Names and addresses are available through ENQUIRY BC (250) 387-6121 or (outside Victoria / within BC) 1-800-663-7867.

Hints and Precautions:

- The rugged 35 km Nootka Trail is a remote destination. All visitors should be self-sufficient. There are many confusing side paths and game trails so it's easy to become disorientated or lost. Carry and use a compass. Consider bringing a portable VHF marine radio for receiving weather updates and for sending emergency messages. Many hikers also pack a small GPS.

- Be prepared for torrential rains at any time of the year. Bring reliable raingear and a good tent with a waterproof fly. Pack everything in plastic bags. Use waterproof covers for your pack and sleeping gear.

- Precise tidal knowledge is essential when hiking the Nootka Trail. Use the *Canadian Tide and Current Tables, Vol. 6*, published by the Canadian Hydrographic Service.

- Gear up for wilderness conditions and allow at least four or five days for your hike.

- Start your day's hiking on a falling tide. Many sections of the beach route are impassable on a flooding or high tide. Some creek and river crossings are only safe (and practical) at low tide. Floats, buoys and markers in the shoreline trees indicate inland trails, beach access points and headland bypass routes.

- The trail traverses a variety of shoreline that includes sandy, pebbled and boulder beaches, slippery, seaweed-covered tidal zones, slick sandstone shelves, irregular peninsulas and rocky ledges. Sections of the inland trail can be extremely muddy. Blowdowns may impede the route. A rope (bring at least 15 m) may be required on some headland bypass trails. Wear good, sturdy footwear.

- Watch for irregular, large and dangerous rogue waves, particularly if you are hiking the shelves and around headlands.

- Boil, treat or filter all water. Availability is dependent on the season and weather.

- Pack out what you carry in and practice no-impact camping. Be careful and sparing with fires. Use a small stove whenever possible.

- Set up your tent well above the high tide line. Choose your campsite carefully to lessen area impact and prevent the contamination of water sources. Leave no trace for future hikers.

- There are no toilets. Bury feces at least 25 cm deep, well removed from water, trails or camp. (Read *Hints and Cautions*, page 15.)

- Hang your food away from camp. Bears and wolves inhabit the area.

- Check with the Department of Fisheries about possible red tide (paralytic shellfish poisoning, or PSP) alerts, permanently closed areas, and spot closures before consuming shellfish. For updates visit www.pac.dfo-mpo.gc.ca. The 24-hour DFO information line is (604) 666-2828 or 1-800-465-4336 (toll-free).

Maps and Guides:

The two topographical maps for the Nootka Trail are NTS 92E/10 Nootka (1:50,000) (which covers the entire trail except the northern tip) and NTS 92E/5 Zeballos (1:50,000) (which shows the trail's north end).

Pal Horvath's *The Nootka Trail: A Backpacker's Guide*, is a concise guide to the Nootka Trail. The booklet has a small-scale general map, contains 13 colour photos, and is filled with camping hints, hiking highlights and descriptions of side routes that over a dozen trips along the trail have revealed. Copies are available for $6.95. Contact (250) 285-2357 for more information. **Special thanks to Pal Horvath for his updates for the Nootka Trail.**

The Federation of Mountain Clubs of BC (FMCBC) publishes an excellent Nootka Trail brochure and map. This informative pamphlet, spearheaded by members of the Alpine Club of Canada (ACC), British Columbia Mountaineering Club (BCMC) and Comox District Mountaineering Club (CDMC), has been instrumental in publicizing the Nootka Trail. Contact them at 47 West Broadway, Vancouver, BC V5Y 1P1 (604) 878-7007; 1-888-892-2266 (toll-free) or visit www.mountainclubs.bc.ca.

For tidal information consult *Canadian Tide and Current Tables, Vol. 6*, published by the Canadian Hydrographic Service, and available at marine and sporting goods stores.

Getting to the Nootka Trail
Air Nootka, Box 19, Gold River, BC V0P 1G0 (250) 283-2255, www.airnootka.com.

Air Nootka provides flights to Louie Bay. Costs are based on type of plane, total weight and number of persons. Rates per trip (2002): Cessna $299.60; Beaver $436.56; Otter $586.36.

Maxi's Water Taxi, Box 1122, Gold River, BC V0P 1G0 (250) 283-2282, provides connections for hikers and kayakers between Gold River and Yuquot / Friendly Cove for $270.00 (2002 rate). Weather permitting you can arrange a water taxi to Louie Bay ($540.00). The boat is a 12-passenger Coast Guard approved vessel.

Nootka Sound Service, (M.V. Uchuck III) Box 57, Gold River, BC V0P 1G0 (250) 283-2515, www.mvuchuck.com. The *MV Uchuck III* offers passenger and freight service to Yuquot / Friendly Cove and Gold River between mid-June and late September, $25.00 one-way (2002 rate).

NOTES:

Map 9A   Nootka Trail (north)

A   Except on extremely low tides, use the inland route.

B   As tides allow, the beach is the usual route. Occasional detours
are required on bypass trails.

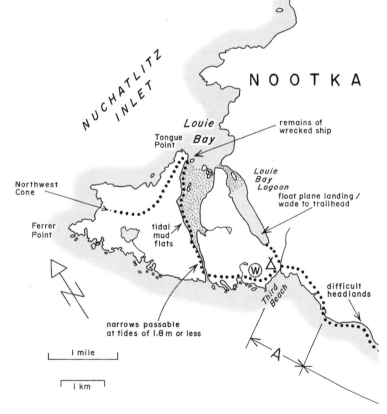

NUCHATLITZ INLET

NOOTKA

Louie Bay

Tongue Point

remains of
wrecked ship

Northwest Cone

Louie Bay Lagoon

float plane landing /
wade to trailhead

Ferrer Point

tidal mud flats

W

Third Beach

difficult headlands

narrows passable
at tides of 1.8 m or less

A

1 mile

1 km

PACIFIC   OCEAN

NOTE: This map is for general reference only. Refer to topographical maps.

Map 9A Nootka Trail (north)

ISLAND

Ewart Lake

Crawfish Lake

Bight
Cone

Calvin Creek

tricky
beach
passage

W

Skuna
Bay

W

Calvin
Falls

B

Map 9B Nootka Trail (south)

C For the most part the trail follows the beach route, with occasional detours on inland bypass trails.

D Use the inland route here. Pocket beaches can be accessed via numerous side trails. Jagged rocky shorelines, impassable headlands and treachous surge channels preclude coastal hiking.

E This section of the Nootka Trail is also part of the Yatz-mahs Trails.

NOTE: This map is for general reference only. Refer to topographical maps.

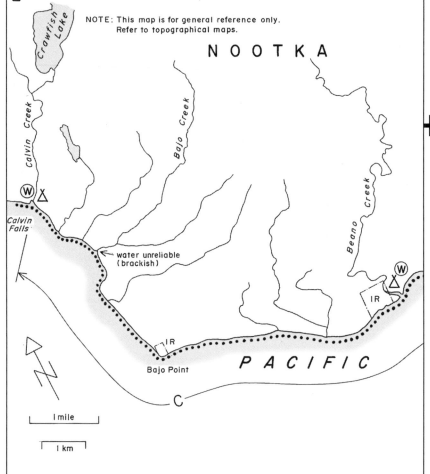

Crawfish Lake

N O O T K A

Calvin Creek

Bajo Creek

Beano Creek

W △

Calvin Falls

← water unreliable (brackish)

I R

W △

I R

Bajo Point

P A C I F I C

C

I mile

I km

NOTES:

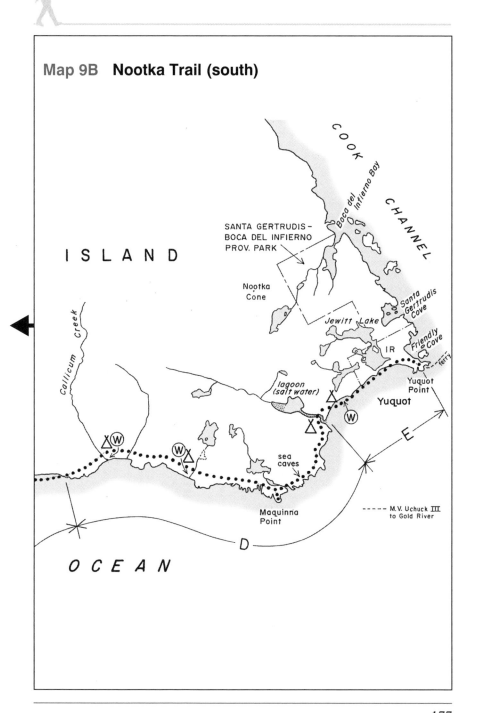

Map 9B **Nootka Trail (south)**

10. Schoen Lake Provincial Park
(Map 10, page 182)

None of the hiking routes described below has received any major work, upgrading, clearing or improvements for over 10 years. These routes are overgrown and route-finding is very difficult, although there are some remnant flags and sections of obvious trail. BC Parks cannot confirm continued services (now provided by a volunteer contractor) at the Schoen Lake campground beyond April 2003. Overnight fees (charged between May 15th and September 30th), $9.00 a campsite (2002 rate.)

Access to Schoen Lake Provincial Park campsite

Refer to Canadian Forest Products' Englewood Division recreational pamphlet. See Map 11 on page 184. For the **Schoen Lake Provincial Park (8689 ha)**, head north on Highway 19, starting at the Sayward Junction. Drive 54.5 km toward Woss and then watch for the Mount Cain / Schoen Lake signposted turnoff, just beyond Croman Lake. Turn left onto Davie Road and follow the park signs another 14 km to the campground. If travelling from Woss, turn right about 10.5 km east of the Woss turnoff. The **Davie River addition (259 ha)** protects old-growth forest on a steep ridge visible as you approach the park from Highway 19. The area is important habitat for elk and deer.

Around 5 km from the Highway 19 cutoff you'll reach a junction. To the left is the access road up to **Mount Cain Regional Park**, described on page 186. The road to Schoen Lake (not recommended for large RVs) roughens as you near the campsite. At Schoen Lake you will find 10 developed campsites and a striking view down the lake of **Mount Schoen**[i] **(1862 m)** and its many peaks.

(a) Schoen Creek Route   (Map 10, page 182)

The Schoen Creek route begins at the most-southerly campsite on Schoen Lake's west shore. Cross the Davie River via a secondary log jam, the main one being at the river's exit from the lake. Use caution at this river crossing. On the south side of the river the hemlock/balsam forest has an imposing primeval quality. Here, the undergrowth is sparse and visibility through the trees is possible for 50 m and more. In other spots the trail is overgrown and obscure.

---

i   The lake and mountain are named after Otto **Schoen**, a former trapper and expert canoe man.

Near the mouth of Schoen Creek, after a 10-minute walk from the trail's last brush with the lakeshore, the hiker will reach the end of the defined route and a junction. (Hiking time from the campsite to this point is around two hours, return.) To the east the route quickly fades, and to the south is a difficult traverse that heads up the Schoen Creek Valley. The valley route has been used for a while and on the east side of Schoen Creek old step-niched logs provide some brief, relatively easy hiking. From here strong hikers could pick their own route up to the saddle. Expect eight hours of steady hiking but the difficult trek is well worth the effort.

(b) Nisnak Lake Route (Map 10, page 182)

A 5 km boat trip or paddle is involved to the head of the Schoen Lake. Water travellers beware! The lake can turn rough in minutes. The Nisnak Lake route has not been maintained and is overgrown and hard to find. It starts from a natural landing site by a grove of big cedars [1] where there are three camping spots. The route, marked by some old blazes and ribbons, runs through a mature hemlock/spruce forest and is more obvious on the south side of Nisnak Creek.

It climbs up on the bench above the creek valley and does not approach the creek until crossing it east of two large alder slides. The alder slides are notable landmarks, and one is at least 200 m wide. Unfortunately, on the north side of the creek, the trail to Nisnak Lake (and also continuing eastwards from it) has many windfalls and is at times difficult to locate. Once through the windfalls the trail meanders through the meadows and isolated stands of timber. Here, it is very well defined and has some muddy and wet parts. From these meadows you can see the five peaks of Mount Schoen and, though too distant to be impressive, Schoen Falls, below the fortress-like South Peak. This is moose-pasture country without the moose. Hiking time from Schoen Lake to Upper Adam Road, five hours, return. Hiking time to Nisnak Meadows: 3.5 hours, return.

Access to Schoen Lake Park from Upper Adam Road

(Map 10, page 182)

The access logging road (Adam River Road) is administered by Weyerhaeuser's North Island Timberlands. Refer to their *Recreation and Logging Road Guide to TFL 39*. There may be active logging in Compton Creek, Adam and Gerald Lake areas. Upper Adam Road is a hauling road, so be aware of heavy industrial traffic. Public access may be restricted on weekdays. In times of very high to extreme fire hazard, the road is closed. Check beforehand with Weyerhaeuser. (See *Logging Companies* on page 24).

From the Sayward Junction, drive north on Highway 19 past Keta Lake and a rest area. Just under 10 km from the Sayward Junction, Upper Adam Road parallels and then crosses Highway 19. **Note: If traffic is heavy it is safer to turn right (north) off Highway 19 and take the logging road bridge back across the highway.** Follow Upper Adam Road for about 21.5 km to a parking area [2] (unsigned) on the left.

A flagged route goes down to the river from here. Be prepared for wet footing and slippery log crossings. The closest camping spot is a single site on the north side of Nisnak Lake (about a 45-minute backpack in). The Nisnak area is dominated by Mount Schoen with its snowfield and waterfalls. The falls drain into the southeastern corner of Nisnak Lake. Although not on a distinct trail, they can be reached by using the drainage route as a guide and by taking advantage of elk trails and traversing the meadows.

The curved ridge that extends southeast from Mount Schoen can be climbed by following the steep gully that points south above the first falls. On the ridge there is easier snow walking and a fine view, and west from the col is a more challenging scramble toward the main peaks of Mount Schoen. (Further south, the long ridge extending east from Mount Adam can be climbed by heading south from Gerald Lake. Allow at least 1 hour to reach the ridge.)

The Compton Creek route can be picked up off the end of Compton Creek Main. The start is hard to find and there are new logging spurs in this area. The route was an old trapline that is overgrown and hard to locate on the ground, but there are still some old blazes. It can be used as a challenging alternative to returning on the Nisnak Trail.

SCHOEN LAKE AND M^T SCHOEN

Rugged mountains form the backdrop at Nisnak Lake, Schoen Lake Provincial Park.

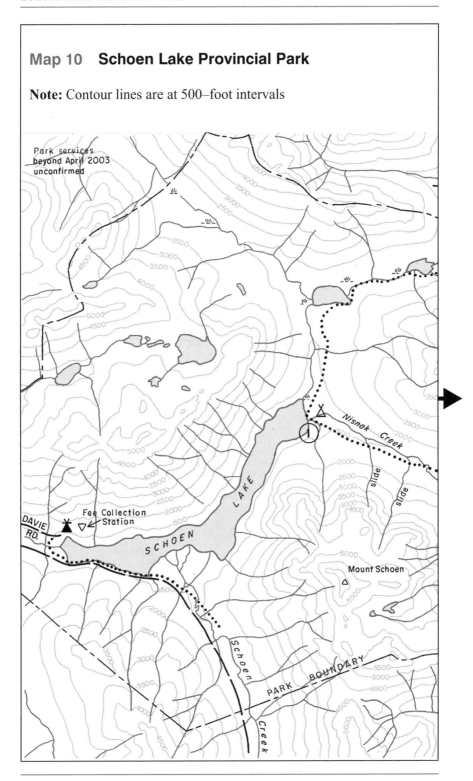

Map 10   Schoen Lake Provincial Park

Note: Contour lines are at 500–foot intervals

Map 10 Schoen Lake Provincial Park

Note: Contour lines are at 500–foot intervals

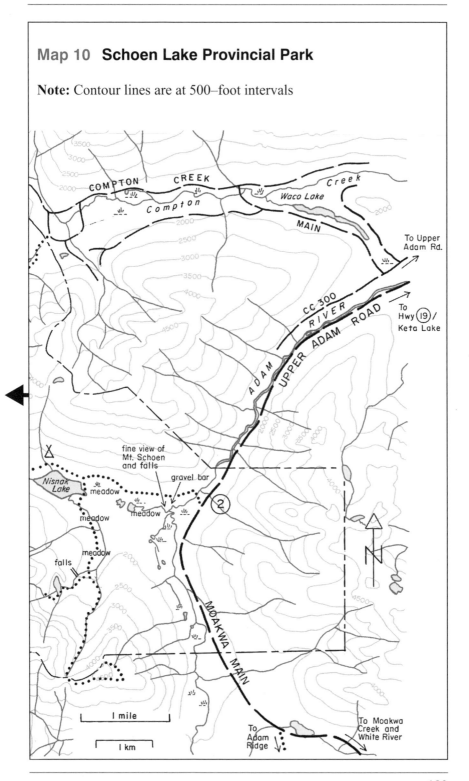

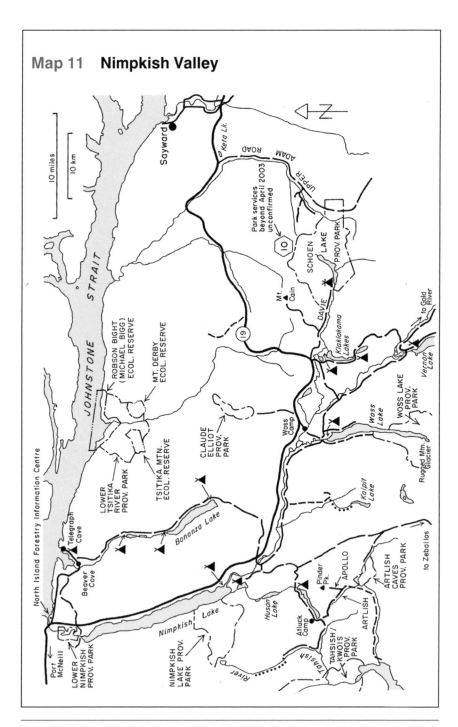

Map 11   Nimpkish Valley

11. Nimpkish Valley
(Map 11, page 184)

When travelling north there are two routes to the Nimpkish Valley:

(a) From Campbell River and Sayward: Highway 19 is paved all the way and enters the Nimpkish Valley near the Klaklakama Lakes.

(b) From Gold River: This 82 km route is via unpaved logging roads. Western Forest Products manages the first section, up to Muchalat Lake. The forests, north of Muchalat Lake all the way up to Beaver Cove, are within Canadian Forest Products' (Canfor) Englewood Division. Follow the logging roads north from Gold River to either Croman Lake or Woss, where the roads connect with Highway 19. (The Croman Lake route via the Klaklakama Lakes is 15 km shorter.)

Contact the Regional District of Mount Waddington in Port McNeill and local logging companies (see page 24.) for current information on area roads and access restrictions. Please light fires only in designated campsites.

(a) Kaipit Lake Fire Route   (Map 11, page 184)

Part of the old fire access trail still exists, but is no longer maintained. This is suitable for strong hikers only. Be prepared for a hefty bushwhack. From Woss Lake recreational campsite, take the Canfor logging road to Nimpkish and about 18 km will bring you to the Kaipit turnoff. It's about 7 km to the trailhead where a difficult creek crossing must be made. This heavily overgrown trail (now more a route than a trail) passes through beautiful but difficult terrain.

(b) Tahsish River Route   (Map 11, page 184)

This obscure route is accessible at various points along the river from Canfor logging roads to the west of Atluck Lake. The trail is prettier upstream. Logging activities could impact parts of the route.

The Nimpkish Valley has several outstanding provincial parks and many hiking and climbing destinations. (See Map 11, on page 184.)

Artlish Caves Provincial Park (254 ha) protects a sensitive area with a future potential as a spelunking destination. Currently, access is extremely difficult and requires travel on Canfor logging roads, where truck hauling is frequent, and a one-kilometre hike up a deactivated road near the park's western boundary. A creek crossing en route is susceptible to sudden and dangerous rises in water levels during heavy rains. This region of karst[i] topography is hazardous due to hidden sinkholes and grikes where a hiker could twist an ankle. No camping is permitted.

Claude Elliot Provincial Park (289 ha) protects a popular angling lake and its surrounding forest. This area is prime elk and deer habitat. Access is just east of Woss from Highway 19 via North Nimpkish Road and Claude Elliot Main. No camping is allowed.

Lower Nimpkish Provincial Park (265 ha) includes a land corridor on both sides of the Lower Nimpkish River that runs 4 km from Nimpkish Lake's north end. Wherever possible, the corridor is 300 m wide from the centre of the river. The Nimpkish River is not part of the park. Access is via the Nimpkish Heights subdivision, south of Port McNeill or by foot or water from the north end of Nimpkish Lake. The Nimpkish River can be hazardous. Wilderness camping is allowed. practice low-impact procedures. There are no developed trails.

Mount Cain Regional Park, accessed along the road to the campsite at Schoen Lake Provincial Park, is primarily a ski area but the cut ski routes are hiked in the summer. Seasonal alpine flowers are a delight. This park is also popular with mountain bikers. From the lodge at the bottom of the ski area (about 16 km from Highway 19), you can hike to the top of **Mount Cain (1646 m)** along a ridge. Expect an elevation gain of a little under 600 m. The park's spectacular mountain backdrop includes Maquilla Peak, Mount Adam and Mount Schoen. For more information contact the Mount Cain Alpine Society at 1-888-688-6622.

Nimpkish Lake Provincial Park (3950 ha) protects the south end of Nimpkish Lake, the most southerly part of the Karmutzen Range's eastern slopes and most of the Tlakwa Creek drainage, excluding some Crown and privately owned land. Access is by water up Nimpkish Lake starting at the boat launch at the Canadian Forest Products' Kim Creek recreation site. This is near the tiny settlement of Nimpkish, along Highway 19, half way between Woss and Port McNeill. Rough foot access is via various Canfor logging roads. Call the logging company for updates on road conditions and entry restrictions. (See *Logging Companies* on page 24.)

---

i   **Karst** (from the name of such a region in Yugoslavia) refers to an area with underground drainage and cavities caused by dissolution of rock. A **grike** is a cleft in a limestone surface that has been widened through solution by carbonation. By extension, a grike can be any cleft in a rock or on a mountain.

Pinder Peak[i] **(1542 m)**, near Atluck Lake, is a rewarding challenge to strong climbers. Steep routes can be accessed by boat across Atluck Lake, or via Artlish Main and Apollo, but a high-clearance four-wheel-drive vehicle is recommended. Access is also possible from an old spur road on Atluck Lake's southeast side. Sections of these Canfor access roads may be impassable by vehicle. Check conditions beforehand with Canfor.

Robson Bight (Michael Bigg) Ecological Reserve (5460 ha) (no public access) is made up of three ecological reserves (Robson Bight, Tsitika Mountain and Mount Derby) and Lower Tsitika River Provincial Park. The reserve was created to provide fragile marine ecosystems in the Robson Bight area. Killer whales use the pebble and smooth rock shores here as rubbing beaches. Whale watching is restricted to Johnstone Strait. The reserve is named after the late Dr. Michael Bigg, a renowned whale researcher.

Tahsish / Kwois Provincial Park (11,022 ha) includes the Tahsish River Ecological Reserve and the area near the head of Kyuquot Sound's Tahsish Inlet. Access to this remote wilderness is by water from Fair Harbour, the Artlish River Valley, Tahsish Inlet and Tahsish River or (from the east) by a rugged hiking route along Canfor logging roads west of Atluck Lake. Expect heavy industrial traffic on these arteries. In early 2001, 193 ha were added to the park to preserve the estuary, pockets of old-growth forest and the natural habitat at the mouth of the Tahsish River.

Woss Lake Provincial Park (6634 ha) includes the south end of Woss Lake, its adjacent forests and the permanent snowfields on the northern face of Rugged Mountain, part of the Haithe Range. **Rugged Mountain (1875 m)**, at the head of Woss Lake, is the highest peak in a compact and impressive group of peaks of interest to alpine climbers both in winter and summer. Traditional access to this area used to be by water via Woss Lake. Few parties enter this way today. Near Zeballos, WFP logging in the Nomash River Valley to the west of Rugged Mountain has extended roads almost to the very base of Rugged Mountain itself. Access is via Nomash Main and the unmarked, overgrown and heavily eroded N20 spur near Nathan Creek.

A steep hike (through large alder in places) and a scramble from the upper part of this spur will allow hikers to reach the main glacier in 3 or 4 hours. To go farther, experience in glacier travel is required. Carry climbing gear, including ice axes, avalanche shovels and even snowshoes. Beware of avalanches. The Rugged Mountain region is prime black bear habitat. There are no facilities and the park is not patrolled or serviced.

---

i   The peak is named after William George **Pinder** (1850-1936), a pioneer land surveyor.

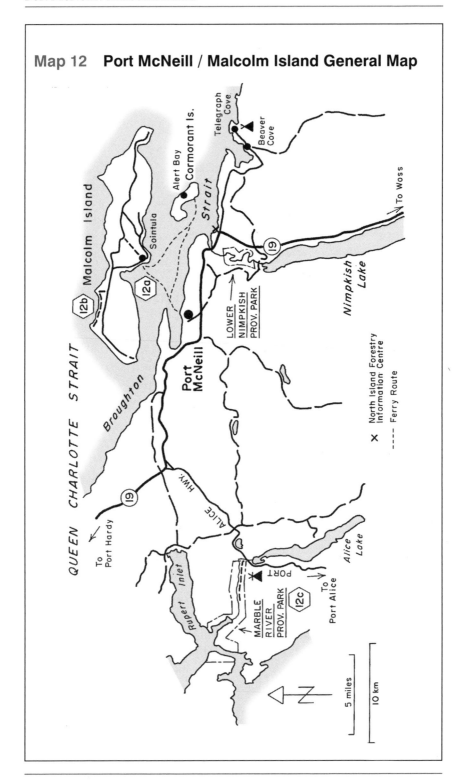

Map 12   Port McNeill / Malcolm Island General Map

12. Port McNeill / Malcolm Island
(Map 12, page 188)

Malcolm Island, just offshore near Port McNeill, was originally settled by Finnish homesteaders at the turn of the 1900s. Sointula celebrated its centennial in 2002. The community's name is a Finnish word meaning "harmony". Two great hiking destinations await Malcolm Island visitors, namely the Mateoja Heritage Trail and the Beautiful Bay Trail. Brochures are available locally. For further information contact: Malcolm Island Tourism, Box 217, Sointula, BC V0N 3E0; Sointula Resource & Info Centre at (250) 973-2001 or visit www.pac.dfo-mpo.gc.ca.

Sointula has a few idiosyncrasies of which non-residents should be aware. The ferry line-up is along 1st Street and the boat scheduled to sail at 8 am actually leaves at 7:30 am. Ferries run between Port McNeill, Malcolm Island and neighbouring Cormorant Island (Alert Bay) about every three hours. Contact BC Ferries at (250) 956-4533 (in Port McNeill), 1-888-223-3779 (toll-free in BC) or www.bcferries.com for schedules.) Sointula's Co-op store and gas station are closed Monday afternoons and all day Sunday.

(a) Mateoja Heritage Trail (Malcolm Island)
From the Sointula ferry dock, take 1st Street to 13th Street and turn right to 3rd Street. Turn left onto 3rd Street, continue almost to its end and turn right to the water tower and the Mateoja Heritage trailhead. (An alternate access to the Big Lake trailhead is via 1st Street, Kaleva Road, Mitchell Bay Road and Big Lake Road.)

The 3.2 km Mateoja Heritage Trail (pronounced "Maat te oy a") traverses the site of a 1923 forest fire and passes an historical homestead dating back to the early 1900s. Little Lake has a picnic site and viewing deck. Other highlights are the marshy area near Melvin's Bog (popular with birdwatchers), the small duck pond, and Big Lake, where there is a picnic site, viewing deck and pit toilet. Big Lake is a popular swimming hole. The trail (rated as moderate) has several benches along the way and ends at the Big Lake Road trailhead. Allow around three hours for a return hike.

(b) Beautiful Bay Trail (Malcolm Island)
The 5.1-kilometre-long Beautiful Bay Trail is located about 6 km from the Sointula ferry dock. Follow 1st Street to Bere Road. Turn right (north) to Pulteney Point Road. Swing left (west) and watch for the Bere Point Campground signs and access road that cuts north to the Beautiful Bay trailhead. Most of the route follows gravel roads. The Bere Point

Campground has eight unserviced campsites and a day-use picnic site. The views of the coastal mountains across Queen Charlotte Strait are striking on a clear day. Be sure to bring drinking water, as there is none at the campground and none available along the trail.

From its start at the Bere Point Campground the trail heads north to Bere Point and then turns along a ridge to parallel Beautiful Bay. Watch for a beach access trail just before the Malcolm Lookout. Next you'll pass the Giant Sitka spruce (64.4 m tall). At the trail's mid-point is Puoli Vali Canyon, site of gold panning in the 1930s. Puoli Vali means "halfway along the journey".

The trail drops off the ridge to the beach (there are some stairs) and crosses a bridge. It then climbs up Lost Canyon via more stairs back to the ridge and the Numas Lookout, about 3.5 km from the trailhead. More stairs lead down to the beach. Just over 5 km from the trailhead, you'll reach Malcolm Point. At low tide you can loop back to the start along the beach. In 2001, over 80 trees fell victim to hurricane-force winds that caused massive blowdowns in the area. Currently (2002), you can only hike as far as Puoli Vali Canyon. Beyond this point, trees still block the route. The trail clearing effort continues.

Allow one hour to Puoli Vali Canyon; 2.5 hours to Malcolm Point; five hours for the return trip. The highest point on the trail is 63.7 m. The Beautiful Bay Trail is rated as moderate with some strenuous sections.

(c) Marble River Trail (Map 12(c), page 191)

From Highway 19, just under 24 km north of the Port McNeill cutoff, take the paved highway towards Port Alice for 14.5 km. Immediately after crossing the Marble River bridge, turn right into a riverside parking area. Leave your vehicle here, and walk in to the campground and follow the signs to the trail. The trail begins at the river, and it takes about one hour to walk to its end.

The Marble River trail offers a pleasant 3.7 km walk through mature hemlock/balsam forest, with access to the river. The trail stays on the bench, above a shallow canyon cut through the limestone rock by the action of the river. It is a very popular recreation spot, especially for steelhead fishing. Bear Falls are a highlight. Watch for American Dippers cavorting around the falls.

Western Forest Products developed the campsite and trail. In 1995, the provincial government set aside the river canyon area, estuary and adjacent lands at Varney Bay and Quatsino Narrows as **Marble River Provincial Park (1512 ha).**

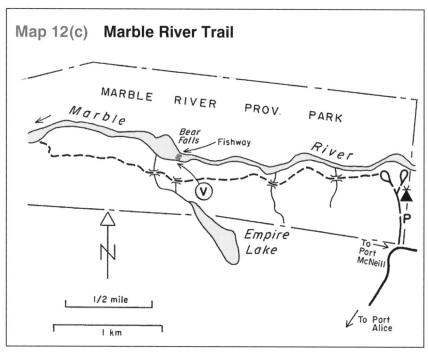

This signpost once marked a logging road junction near Holberg.

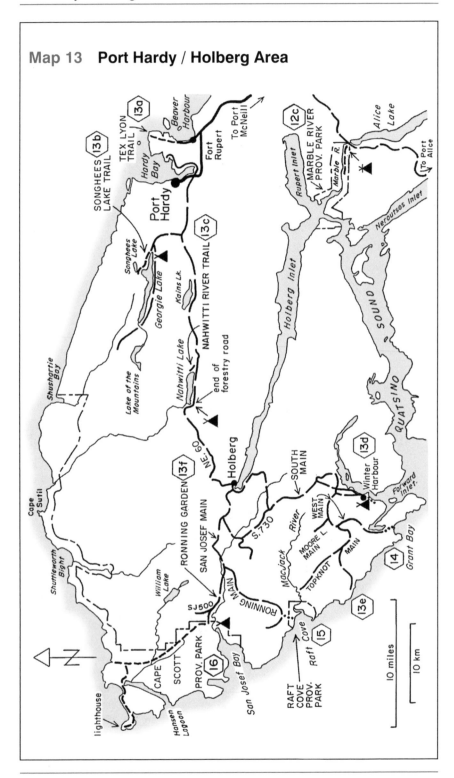

Map 13   Port Hardy / Holberg Area

13. Port Hardy / Holberg Area
(Map 13, page 192)

To reach Cape Scott and Raft Cove provincial parks or Grant Bay and the Winter Harbour area, take the signposted Holberg Road from Highway 19, about 2 km before you reach Port Hardy. The gravel road from Port Hardy to Holberg (45.5 km) is generally in good to fair condition but the route is narrow and winding. Active logging may be encountered the whole way, so watch for loaded logging trucks and heavy industrial traffic. Keep your vehicle's headlights on and anticipate meeting a truck at every turn. Western Forest Products logging trucks, crew vehicles and industrial traffic have right-of-way. Currently (2002) access is open 24 hours a day, but check with WFP's Holberg office for current hauling updates, road conditions and safest travel times. Refer to WFP's *Visitors Guide to Logging Roads and Recreation Areas (Northern Vancouver Island Region)*. Copies are usually available at local logging offices in Port McNeill or Holberg (see *Logging Companies* on page 24), and at travel infocentres. This map shows current active logging areas as well as recently built roads and deactivated spurs. This map also details access to Cape Scott, Raft Cove, Grant Bay and over a dozen other major recreation sites.

Holberg has a gas station (hours of operation vary), a neighbourhood pub and a motel. To get from Holberg to Winter Harbour, West Main and Topknot Main, follow South Main to Winter Harbour (about 25.5 km).

See page 135 for a photograph of Winter Harbour.

(a) Tex Lyon Trail (Map 13, page 192)

This rugged, 7 km trail to Dillon Point features rocky headlands along the shores of historic Beaver Harbour, east of Port Hardy. Hikers access the trail by parking at the public park area in Beaver Harbour. The trailhead is near the boat launch. A short walk along a beautiful sandy beach brings the hiker to a rock bluff. Watch the tides, as there is a creek that flows past the bluff and access at high tide is over a log jam on the creek, above the high tide line. At low tide it's relatively easy to hop across the creek at a narrow spot. For tidal information consult *Canadian Tide and Current Tables, Vol. 6*, available from marine and sporting goods stores. Cross the bluff carefully, as there are a variety of wildflowers and other plants that grow only in this xeric (dry) microenvironment.

Be prepared for a rugged and challenging hike. There are picnic tables and rest areas along the way. Basket Eaters' Cove is approximately the halfway point. This is a great destination to view a variety of bird, forest and marine life and the seascapes of Beaver Harbour and Queen Charlotte Strait. Signs mark the route. Hiking times (one way): 20 minutes to the bluff; 2 hours, 20 minutes to Basket Eaters' Cove; or 4.5 hours to Dillon Point. While there is an ongoing maintenance program on the trail, it is not always easy to get through the ubiquitous growth of northern Vancouver Island salal.

The trail is administered and maintained through the Regional District of Mount Waddington and the Port Hardy Lions Club. A trail brochure is available. Further details can be obtained by calling Development Services at the Regional District of Mount Waddington, (250) 956-3301.

(b) Songhees Lake Trail   (Map 13, page 192)

From Highway 19, near Port Hardy, take the Cape Scott / Holberg / Winter Harbour cutoff and continue about 7 km to the Georgie Lake Forest Service Road (FSR). Turn right and follow this seasonally good gravel road another 5 km to Georgie Lake. Loaded logging trucks may use this road (see page 193.) At Georgie Lake there is a sandy beach, and a BCFS camp-ground with 5 campsites and pit toilets. The Songhees Lake Trail, an angler's route, leads about 5 km from the campsite to Songhees Lake. The lure is good cutthroat trout fishing. The trail is suitable for all age groups but can be overgrown in spots.

(c) Nahwitti River Trail   (Map 13, page 192)

As you approach Port Hardy, take the Cape Scott / Holberg / Winter Harbour cutoff along Highway 19. Follow Holberg Road (see page 193) for approximately 24.5 km to the parking area, on the right (north) side of the road, just east of Nahwitti Lake. The Nahwitti River Trail winds 2 km alongside the river and through a serene old-growth forest to a tiny pocket beach on Nahwitti Lake.

(d) Botel Park Trail   (Map 13, page 192)

Take Holberg Road from Port Hardy to Holberg (see page 193.) From Holberg take South Main a further 25.5 km to Winter Harbour. The Botel Park Trail begins near the end of the road in Winter Harbour. Check with WFP's Holberg office for current hauling information and safe travel times.

From the small parking area, wooden stairs lead to the trail that meanders through an old-growth forest to a rocky beach on Forward Inlet. Time your hike for lower tides so you can include a beach hike to the southwest. (Use the *Canadian Tide and Current Tables: Volume 6*.) Watch your step on the often-slippery beach stones. Hike as far as you can until a jagged headland impedes further progress. Here you'll discover a vantage point from which you can gaze down Forward Inlet and the entrance of Quatsino Sound. On a clear day you can make out the distant shape of Brooks Peninsula.

(e) Hecht Beach Trail (Map 13, page 192)

Follow the route directions listed for Grant Bay, page 196. At the West Main/Topknot Main junction, stay on Topknot Main for approximately 11 km, then turn left, onto Hecht Main and continue another 5 km to where the road stops. This secondary road has been deactivated and roughens as you approach its end. Watch for the trailhead, on the left and the short coastal trail to rugged Hecht Beach. Active logging on area mainlines may restrict public access. See page 193, and check with WFP's Holberg office for current hauling information and safest travel times. (See *Logging Companies* on page 24.)

(f) Ronning Garden (Map 13, page 192)

As you approach Port Hardy, take the Cape Scott / Holberg / Winter Harbour cutoff from Highway 19 and head west on Holberg Road (see page 193.) Once you reach Holberg, take the San Josef Main, following the signs for Cape Scott Provincial Park. (See page 203.) Around 59 km from Highway 19 (about 1 km past the Ronning Main / Raft Cove Provincial Park cutoff) watch for the Ronning Garden sign and turn right (north) to a small parking area. Turning around here can be a problem so leave room for others. Walk 15 minutes west along the cleared old wagon road to the Ronning Garden.

The Ronning Garden is located on land originally settled by Norwegian Bernt Ronning in 1910. He cleared 2 ha of rainforest and started an exotic garden of imported plants from around the world. The old wagon road from San Josef Bay and the Cape Scott settlement ran by his place and, with an upstairs floor custom-made for dancing, and a pump organ below, it's no wonder many travellers made the Ronning homestead a frequent stop. Ronning lived there until the early 1960s.

Many of his plantings still survive, including giant rhododendrons, Japanese cedars, Mexican bamboo and two large monkey puzzle trees that once guarded his house (now collapsed). Turn to page 134 for a photo of the cabin as it appeared in the 1970s. The current owners have spent years clearing, restoring and identifying the garden. Their tireless efforts continue. Please contribute generously at the donation box near the information sign. Contact (250) 288-3724 for more details.

14. Grant Bay

(Map 14, page 197)

Grant Bay is an isolated little bay on the north side of the entrance to Quatsino Sound. Bounded by a shoreline of shoals and rock, its main attraction is 800 m of sandy beach. Hiking time one way: under half an hour by land route or about one hour by the sea route, not including water travel time from Winter Harbour.

Winter Harbour, about 25.5 km from Holberg, is a quaint little fishing village complete with a boardwalk, well-kept old houses, three wharves, a store, restaurant, and a hotel. Just north of the village is the Regional District of Mount Waddington's Kwaksistah seaside campsite guarded by a brightly coloured, eagle-topped totem pole.

Land Access: See Map 13 on page 192, the ***Port Hardy / Holberg Area*** section on page 193 and ***Logging Roads*** on page 24.

From the signposted Highway 19 junction, 2 km south of Port Hardy, take Holberg Road and travel 45.5 km to Holberg (see page 193.) From Holberg, follow South Main, a main haul road, for 22 km and turn right at the West Main / South Main junction, just north of Winter Harbour. After travelling about 6 km on West Main, at the junction with Topknot Main, take the left fork and continue south on West Main to cross Kwatleo Creek. Follow posted signs to the trailhead. WFP has extended West Main south towards Grant Bay. The logging road cuts west (to cross Kwatleo Creek again), turns south, and eventually runs due east to the new Grant Bay parking area.

The Grant Bay Trail was re-established by WFP in the late 1990s. From the parking area it's under half an hour to the shining smooth sands of Grant Bay. The trail is a popular route for black bears; Grant Bay and Browning Inlet are preferred hangouts for them. Bears are unlikely to be a problem as they are genuinely wild and associate people with danger and not with food. The trail winds southeast through a forest of spruce and hemlock, with very large spruce trees. Sword fern, deer fern and salmonberry are common plants.

Facing south, Grant Bay is somewhat protected from the open Pacific, and its surf is moderate compared to the exposed west coast beaches. From the beach you can see Cape Parkins, Kwakiutl Point and Cape Cook at the end of Brooks Peninsula. Shore travel and rock scrambling any distance from the Grant Bay beach is difficult; the adjacent shores are all rock. Just relax and enjoy the sand and sun while watching the freighters and fish boats pass by.

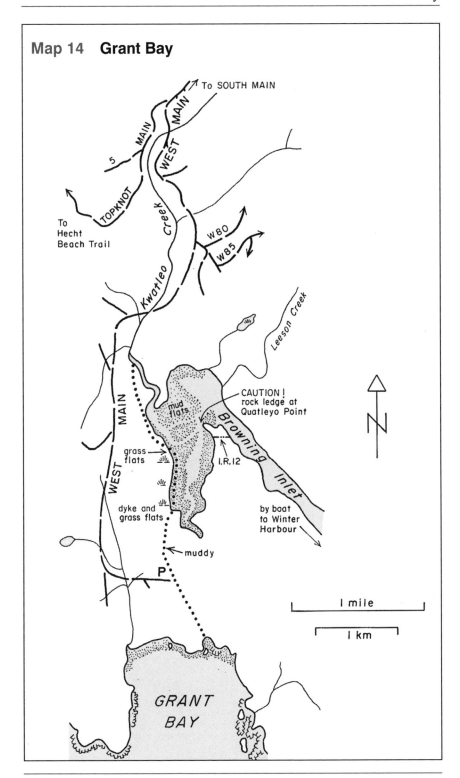

Map 14 **Grant Bay**

To SOUTH MAIN

MAIN

WEST MAIN

5

TOPKNOT

To
Hecht
Beach Trail

Kwatleo Creek

W80

W85

Leeson Creek

CAUTION!
rock ledge at
Quatleyo Point

N

WEST MAIN

mud
flats

Browning Inlet

grass
flats

I.R.12

dyke and
grass flats

by boat
to Winter
Harbour

muddy

P

1 mile

1 km

GRANT
BAY

Water is available from the stream at the west end of the beach. This is poor-tasting cedar water, but drinkable and should be boiled, filtered or treated. The stream mouth is jammed with sea logs. Tents should be placed high on the beach, safely above the high tide mark.

The trail north from the parking area to Browning Inlet (part of the water-access route) is lined by thick salal and is usually muddy. It winds through a spike-topped cedar/hemlock forest with scattered large balsams. The route emerges in the southwest corner of the inlet and is marked by plastic jugs in an old fruit tree. This old tree and its neighbours, together with a dyke, are the epitaphs to a failed attempt at cultivation. The 50-centi-metre-high dike extends into the grassy fringe north and east from the forest for 80 m and 90 m respectively.

Walk north on the relatively firm tidal mud rather than the grassy fringe, which has many small but hazardous natural ditches. You can follow an overgrown route north from the inlet to parallel Kwatleo Creek for about 35 minutes. Encroaching salmonberry crowds the trail near the mouth of the creek. The forest here is spruce and cedar.

Water Access: From Winter Harbour, launch a small boat, canoe or kayak and head down Forward Inlet, then northwest up Browning Inlet. This is a distance by sea of 9 km. Philip Stooke warns, in his book (long out of print) *Landmarks and Legends of the North Island*, that at high tide at Quatleyo Point (the tip of the First Nations Reserve) there is an extensive hidden rock ledge which must be avoided. He recommends landing near the north end of the bay. However, if planning to return at high tide, the boater will be able to get within 220 m of the start of the Browning Inlet / parking area section of the trail. The route from the inlet to the parking area is usually muddy and overgrown with salal. The hike to Grant Bay from Browning Inlet takes just under an hour. Sturdy boots are an advantage.

NOTES:

A rugged trail winds in to a sandy beach at Raft Cove Provincial Park.

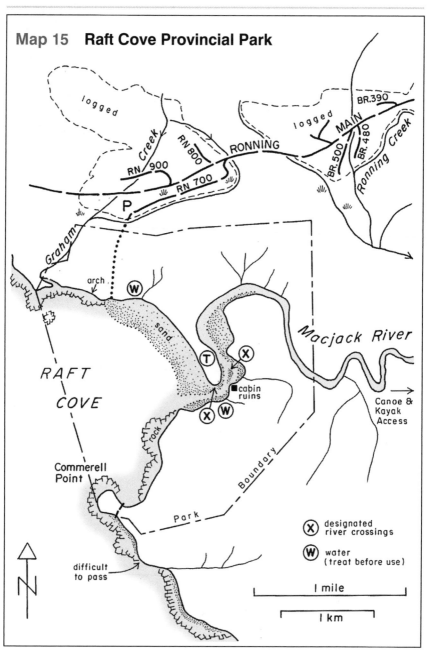

Map 15   Raft Cove Provincial Park

15. Raft Cove Provincial Park

(Map 15, page 200)

Isolated on the northwest coast of Vancouver Island, south of Cape Scott Park, Raft Cove Provincial Park is distinguished by its 1.3 km length of open sandy beach. The cove offers little protection from the winds, and the Pacific surf pounds its shores relentlessly. The Macjack River meanders into the ocean at the south end of the beach. A narrow but forested peninsula separates the Pacific on the west from the Macjack River on the east.

Access: See Map 13 on page 192. To get to Raft Cove Provincial Park, take Holberg Road from the junction along Highway 19 as you approach Port Hardy. Access is via active logging roads. Read the section *Port Hardy / Holberg Area*, on page 193. WFP's *Visitor's Guide to Logging Roads and Recreation Areas (Northern Vancouver Island Region)* is a useful adjunct.

Travel 45.5 km to Holberg, then continue on San Josef Main and follow the signposts for Raft Cove and Cape Scott provincial parks. A little over 12 km past Holberg (58 km from Highway 19) cut west onto Ronning Main (signposted for Raft Cove Provincial Park). Swing left onto a spur road (Ronning 700) about 10 km from San Josef Main. Drive to the end of the secondary road to the parking area. There is limited parking here.

Route to Raft Cove   (Map 15, page 200)

The route to Raft Cove takes 45 minutes to hike and begins near the parking area. The rugged route winds about 1.4 km to the beach through mature forests. The first part cuts through WFP forestlands. This route receives minimal maintenance and hikers should exercise care and caution as you'll encounter muddy sections and downed trees that you must climb over, walk on or crawl under.

The cabin on the south side of the Macjack is Willie Hecht's old trapping cabin. It is mouse-ridden and in disrepair. According to L.R. Peterson's *Cape Scott Story,* Hecht and the Boytle family were the pioneers of the Macjack settlement in 1913, but by the early 'twenties only Hecht was left. As early as 1909 a trail had been established from Raft Cove up Ronning Creek to the San Josef Bay / Holberg trail.

Summer tenters will enjoy camping on Raft Cove beach. Here there is crashing surf, passing freighters and distant fish boats silhouetted against the horizon. The best water is available from the stream emptying into the south side of the Macjack near the old cabin, although fresh water is also available at the north end of the beach. Remember to boil, treat or filter all cooking and drinking water. There is a food cache approximately at the midpoint of the beach and another closer to the south end. Please use these food caches since bears and other wildlife are common. There is also a pit toilet near the beach's south end.

Canoe and kayak access is possible via the Macjack River from the Winter Harbour road systems. Take South Main from Holberg Inlet, turn onto West Main and then onto Topknot Main. The short spur road (deactivated) to the Macjack River leaves Topknot Main just under 19 km from Holberg. There is a short 50 m hike to the river. The Macjack is influenced by the tide at this point so plan accordingly, using the *Canadian Tide and Current Tables, Vol. 6.*

During low tides, shore walks can be made both north and south of Raft Cove. To the south, where small islands of jagged tidal rock stand in sharp contrast to the sands of Raft Cove, an easy 2.2 km walk is possible. South of Commerell Point you'll encounter extremely slippery rocks and a steep slope overgrown with salal. Commerell Point itself can be crossed at its neck by a bypass trail.

Evidence of the ruins of the first Hansen Lagoon dike lies close to the Fisherman River at Cape Scott Provincial Park.

16. Cape Scott Provincial Park

(Map 16A, page 204 / Map 16B, page 206)

Cape Scott Provincial Park[i] is a rugged, remote area, where hurricane-force winds and deluging rains can occur at any time of the year. Torrential downpours may last for days. Trails are often muddy. Hikers should be properly equipped for and familiar with wilderness travel. Gear up for extreme conditions. During the summer (June through September) there is an overnight camping fee in place for all backcountry camping in Cape Scott Provincial Park. In 2002 this fee is $5 per person (16 years of age and older), per night.

See Map 13 on page 192. From the signposted junction along Highway 19, approximately 2 km south of Port Hardy, take Holberg Road and travel 45.5 km to Holberg. Continue on San Josef Main and follow the Cape Scott Provincial Park signposts. The Cape Scott / San Josef Bay trailhead is at the end of San Josef Main, about 18.5 km from Holberg (65 km from Highway 19). The entrance to WFP's San Josef campsite is one kilometre before the trailhead. There is parking space at the start of the trail, but on busy weekends vehicles line the roadway. When parking, do not block other cars.

On the logging roads, give way to all heavy logging vehicles as they have right of way, and drive with your lights on so you can be seen through the dust clouds. There are several logging company and BCFS campsites in the area. Refer to WFP's *Visitors Guide to Logging Roads and Recreation Areas (Northern Vancouver Island Region)*.

You would need at least a week or more in the area to see everything at **Cape Scott Provincial Park (22,131 ha)**. The whole park is a naturalist's paradise. Most of the trails are the old settlers' roads, some of which were cleared out by the former CFS Holberg Ground Search Team as a 1971-72 Centennial Project. The park was established in 1973. BC Parks' staff does seasonal upgrading. The **Cape Scott Trail**, now 23.6 km long, follows the settlers' trails and an old telegraph line that ran from Holberg Inlet northwest to Fisherman Bay, Hansen Lagoon and the Cape Scott lighthouse. The old telegraph wire can still be seen in some locations.

The first part of the trail is in the Quatsino Rain Forest (annual rainfall between 380 cm and 510 cm) so here the trail is always muddy. The weather improves towards Cape Scott, but is always unpredictable and it can be downright chilly even in summer. Always be prepared for the unexpected and gear up for extreme conditions.

---

i   David Scott was a principal backer of the trading voyage made by James Strange in 1786.

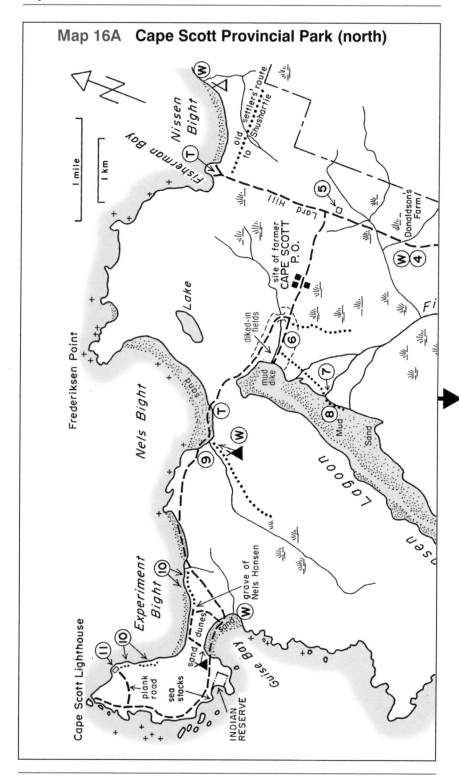

Map 16A Cape Scott Provincial Park (north)

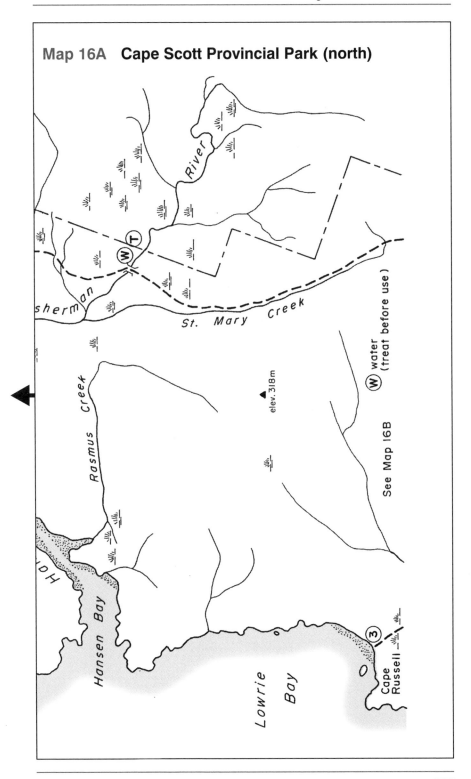

Map 16A Cape Scott Provincial Park (north)

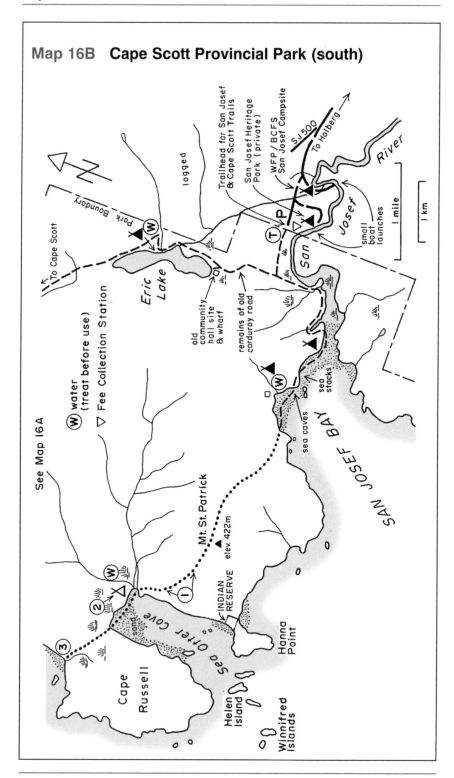

Map 16B Cape Scott Provincial Park (south)

Distances and approximate hiking times in good weather from the parking lot.

	km	hours	
San Josef Bay	2.5	¾	water, camping, pit toilets
Eric Lake	3	1	fresh water, camping, pit toilets, food caches
Fisherman River	9.3	3	water, pit toilet
Nissen Bight	15	5.5	water at the east end, camping, pit toilet, food cache
Hansen Lagoon	14.7	5	
Nels Bight	16.8	6	good camping area, water at the south end, pit toilets, Ranger Station, food caches
Experiment Bight	18.9	6.5	
Guise Bay	20.7	7	limited water, camping, pit toilets, food cache
Cape Scott	23.6	8	lighthouse

Notations for circled numbers on Cape Scott Park maps:

1. Very steep section.
2. Campsite and water. Grasses are awash at high tide.
3. Interesting forest, large burls and water.
4. Old farm site and water.
5. Christensen boy's grave in grove of trees by holly bushes.
6. Hansen Lagoon, subject to high tides.
7. Log crossing, submerged at high tide.
8. Remnants of original settlers' dike, now washed-out.
9. Ranger cabin, staffed in the summer months.
10. Headland by-pass routes.
11. Supply landing.

The Cape Scott area is of immense historical interest, and the informative, historical interpretive signs at various locations in the park are well worth reading. Opened up by sturdy Danish settlers in the late 1890s, this was the scene of toil and disillusionment. The settlers were gradually defeated in their efforts to homestead the land by the many hardships: the impossibility of getting produce to market, failure of the governments of the day to provide the promised road, stormy winters which made it difficult to land supply boats, cougars which devoured their domestic animals, and lack of medical help in emergencies.

But many of the settlers' clearings, roads and buildings are still visible for the hiker to marvel at. Most homes are now flat and all equipment has been removed except for the rusting remains of the heaviest implements. The one-time farmlands are deserted. There are countless side trails and old farm sites to discover — in fact, as many things as you have time to hunt for. Use caution when exploring these sites; many of the settlers' wells still lie hidden and there may be broken glass and rusty nails scattered about. Old standing structures are unstable.

A good one-day hike may be made to San Josef Bay and as far as Eric Lake. Anyone venturing further in should be properly equipped with backpacking gear and food. Taking several days to camp and explore this area is an excellent trip. About 1 km west of the trailhead the trail forks. To the right (north) is the main Cape Scott Trail and the turn for Eric Lake. Keep left at the junction for one kilometre to **San Josef Bay** and its beautiful wildlife marshes and expanses of sandy beaches. Most of the trail to San Josef is surfaced with gravel, well graded and wheelchair accessible.

You can canoe or kayak down the San Josef River all the way to the surf at San Josef Bay. You need favourable sea and wind conditions and, because the river is affected by tides, you have to be precise in calculating river tides. A good flood tide eliminates many of the rapids and shallows that develop on an ebb tide. Be ready to portage and line. Put in at the WFP campsite or from the BC Parks boat launch. The latter is reached at San Josef Heritage Park, at the end of the spur road, halfway between the WFP campsite and the Cape Scott / San Josef Bay trailhead. Both of these water access points are suitable for canoes and small cartop boats.

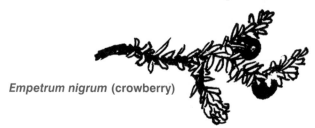

Empetrum nigrum (crowberry)

At the far end of San Josef Bay, a rough route climbs to the top of **Mount St. Patrick (422 m)**, which affords a magnificent viewpoint. The summit is covered with crowberry[i] and there are some swampy sections. From here the trail leads to **Sea Otter Cove**, approximately 10 km. Allow about 2½ hours, one way. Currently this trail has had little if any work done on it, except for the occasional clearing of windfalls. Faded markers can be found on some trees. Fresh water is at the cove, but you must bushwhack up the creek about 100 m to go above the tides. The route around the head of Sea Otter Cove is passable only at mid- to low tide. From here it is about 2 km to **Lowrie Bay** where you'll find fresh water and high-tide beach camping. Anyone contemplating this rugged route should carry the topographical map NTS 102 I/9 San Josef (1:50,000), and a compass.

From the San Josef Bay Trail junction, hike north, on the main **Cape Scott Trail**, to the first campsite from the trailhead, at **Eric Lake**. BC Parks has installed 13 tent pads, fire rings, food caches and a pit toilet. This is a scenic treasure, with warm swimming and cutthroat trout fishing only metres away on the gravel bar at the mouth of the creek running into Eric Lake.

Fisherman River has a good log bridge (and pit toilet) but you should be careful at some of the other creek crossings. Farther on you come to the signposted turn-off to Hansen Lagoon and Nels Bight. The trail north to Nissen Bight continues through fairly open country of sphagnum bogs with cedar and hemlock small-growth vegetation, then down "Lard Hill" (very slippery clay soil in some places) through timber to Fisherman Bay and Nissen Bight. **Fisherman Bay** is a gravelled bay with an old wooden shipwreck; **Nissen Bight** is made up of 800 m of clean white sand, with relatively small, evergreen growth to the foreshore. Remnants of the old Shushartie route eastwards can be found with some difficulty a short distance beyond the clay stretch of the trail bed. A tough bushwhack leads about 1.5 km to the remains of a 340-metre-long bridge over a lake.

Returning to the Hansen Lagoon / Nels Bight turn-off, hike to the site of the former Cape Scott Post Office and farm (burned down in 1971), past the remains of the old community hall and down to the several hundred hectares of flat meadowland at **Hansen Lagoon**. These are of special interest to any visitor as they were diked by the settlers with rock and fill to keep out the tidal waters. Remnants of breached dikes still remain. The lagoon, part of the Pacific Flyway, is a seasonal habitat for migrating Canada geese and other waterfowl.

---

i   *Empetrum nigrum* (from the Greek for 'in rock' and 'black') is variously known as crowberry, curlew berry and crakeberry (*crake* is Old Norse for crow), possibly because of the glossy black drupes (berries), which are popular with birds and bears, but not with some people.

To get to the big surf beach, Nels Bight, take the trail to the right at the BC Parks sign as you reach the lagoon meadow. **Nels Bight** has nearly 2 km of flat white sand with pounding surf. At the west end of the beach there is a good water supply although **BC Parks advises that ALL park water should be treated, filtered or boiled before use.** Pit toilets have also been installed at two locations here as shown on our map. The ranger cabin is not for public use, but is a seasonal base for park rangers.

From Nels Bight the trail to the lighthouse climbs in behind an impassable headland and drops back to the beach at **Experiment Bight**, with its sandy shore and rolling breakers. Walk through thick salal on an old plank road to **Guise Bay**, another beautiful surf beach. At Guise Bay there are the remains of an old RCAF installation from W.W.II. From there go north through sand dunes to the jeep road leading uphill for about 2 km through lush vegetation to the lighthouse, the final destination. Read the notice board at the lighthouse. The Cape Scott lighthouse was built in 1960 and is still staffed.

You once could hike farther, out to the very tip of Vancouver Island. First you went through the gate, near the lighthouse, and down a series of seemingly endless steps and wooden staircases. (Editor's Note: I tried counting the stairs a couple of times and never reached the same figure twice. Suffice to say there were hundreds of steps – and you had to climb back up on your return.) Next you negotiated a slick, damp boardwalk and then crossed a couple of jagged tidal rock cuts on two swaying cable suspension bridges. Another stretch of wooden boardwalk extended to the Cape Scott foghorn. From here, a final scramble through thick salal led to a log, behind which you could shelter from the almost-incessant winds, and watch the waters beneath you churn and roil, as angry seas challenged defiant headlands. What was a spectacular highlight of any journey to Cape Scott is now a part of park history. The trail, stairs, boardwalk and two lofty suspension bridges were closed by the federal government and removed in 1999.

On returning to Guise Bay, walk across the sand dunes back to the northern shore, and return to **Experiment Bight** by trail along the beach past lovely little rocky coves, to make your hike at the Cape into a round trip. Hanging floats mark headland bypass routes. (Note: By going down the plank side road to the supply landing and out to the end of the longest guy wire, you can find a primitive trail to the beach and return to the sand neck by beaches and headland by-pass trails.) Be alert for black bears.

The BC Parks Cape Scott Provincial Park pamphlet contains many useful hints and pre-trip planning tips. Copies are available at tourist infocentres.

Pick one up soon. When current stocks run out these brochures won't be reprinted. Additional information can be found at the BC Parks website. (See **BC Parks** on page 23.)

You must be completely self-sufficient from Holberg onwards. Come well prepared and have a good week's supply of food. Help may be available from the Ranger Station at Nels Bight during the summer months. Only in extreme emergency could assistance be forthcoming from the lighthouse. Though you may visit around the lighthouse at Cape Scott, do not expect any hospitality from the staff there. The lighthouse water supply is rainwater caught in cisterns, so they have no water to spare.

Torrential rains, sometimes lasting for days, can occur at any time of the year. Pack everything in plastic bags. Carry a rainproof tent, dependable raingear, waterproof matches, firestarter, a small stove, change of clothing and socks, and, in summer, bug repellent. Plenty of warm dry clothing is more useful than a pair of heavy binoculars. Polypropylene, fleece or wool clothing will keep you warm even when wet. A rain suit, taped at the ankles, helps to keep the mud at bay. Sturdy boots with good support, and gaiters are essential for the mud (no running shoes), and even with that combination, some people prefer to hike in shorts to stay cool. High-topped leather or rubber boots are other options.

Beach hiking can be dangerous and is not recommended because many headlands are impassable. Knowledge of tides is essential. Coastal travel should not be attempted on a high or incoming tide. If you camp on a beach, be careful to pitch your tent well above the high-water mark. When backed by a wind, the incoming tides tend to be higher than is shown in the tide book. If you are planning to use the beaches, bring the tide table **Canadian Tide and Current Tables, Vol. 6**, published by the Canadian Hydrographic Service.

During the summer, the salt marsh flats at Hansen Lagoon offer a good growth of goose tongue (plantain) grass. Look for the succulent "sea asparagus" which, when added to soup and stews, forms a good dietary supplement to freeze-dried food. Salmonberries, huckleberries and salal berries are plentiful in summer.

The mussels on the beaches, though a bit tough, are edible. There are no clams or oysters. Check with the Department of Fisheries about red tide (paralytic shellfish poisoning, or PSP) alerts, permanently closed areas, and spot closures before consuming any shellfish. For updates visit www.pac.dfo-mpo.gc.ca. The 24-hour DFO information line is (604) 666-2828 or 1-800-465-4336 (toll-free). If you plan on fishing, be aware of current provincial or federal regulations and obtain the proper freshwater or saltwater licenses prior to your hike.

Hints and Precautions:

- Secure your vehicle and leave no valuables inside. Parking areas are not patrolled.

- Carry NTS topographical maps (1:50,000) 102 I/9 San Josef, 102 I/16 Cape Scott.

- Pack reliable rain gear. Wear sturdy boots that offer good support.

- Keep to designated trails to help minimize damage to fragile vegetation and soil structure.

- Exercise caution when traversing wooden boardwalks. They can be dangerously slick when wet or damp.

- Use a hiking staff to probe mudholes, quagmires and boggy areas.

- Floats and buoys hanging in trees indicate beach access points and headland bypass routes.

- Bring insect repellent, antidotes for bites, and a first aid kit.

- Pack in a portable stove and extra fuel. Suitable firewood is in short supply. Build only small driftwood and downed-wood fires.

- Choose your campsite carefully, to avoid high tides and dangerous trees. Random camping is permitted, but BC Parks suggests sticking to established sites, to lessen area impact and prevent the contamination of water sources. Dismantle all temporary shelters completely so there is no trace of them for future visitors.

- Leave all campsites as you would like to find them, clean and with a supply of dry wood for the next comers. Take your litter out with you and leave nothing to attract bears and small animals.

- Cougars and black bears (even wolves) inhabit the park's forests and shorelines. Hang your food at night and when you are away from camp. Use the bear-proof food caches where they are provided.

- Wash in the ocean, whenever possible, even if you use biodegradable soap. Otherwise stay 30 m away from streams and lakes.

- If there are no pit toilets dig a hole at least 30 m from lakes and streams. Please ensure that you bury all excrement and burn toilet paper.

- Keep dogs on a leash.

- Respect all private property, First Nations Reserves and historical sites within the Park. Don't remove artifacts.

- Firearms are prohibited within the Park except during a valid hunting season.

- In 1995 the **Nahwitti / Shushartie coastal corridor (6750 ha)** was added to Cape Scott Provincial Park. In 2001 the corridor was increased by another 282 ha. The establishment of a North Coast Trail from Cape Scott Park east to Port Hardy is a future consideration.

Tide–created standing waves form a backdrop for a hiker along the San Josef River.

Index

A Postscript

When this edition of Hiking Trails III went to print, management of outdoor recreation on public lands was changing significantly, notably within the organizational structures, roles and capabilities of both BC Parks and the BC Forest Service. For example, by the time you read this book, some offices we have mentioned may be slated for closure, or they may have already been closed; perhaps others may have been opened. We just don't know at this point, and we are unable to predict with any certainty.

Some provincial park management, including campgrounds, may be privatized or transferred to municipalities and regional districts, but these changes will not affect the trails and routes described in this book. A greater reliance on 'no trace' camping practices and 'self maintenance' may be needed, but these have been and should remain reasonable models to follow. Road access, however, may change significantly. Volunteers and not-for-profit organizations may play a greater role in park and outdoor recreation management. It appears to be policy to close facilities that require servicing, resulting in the removal of outhouses, non-availability of safe water, lack of firewood, etc. Charges may be made for services that previously were publicly funded.

VITIS has confidence in the reliability of information about the hiking trails and backcountry routes presented in this volume as of publication date. However, the pace and scope of change makes uncertain the information regarding management agencies, organizational arrangement, the provision of services and maintenance of facilities.

Hikers are encouraged to check with the contacts suggested in the book before venturing where there are uncertainties. Hikers are also encouraged to check our website for changes, and to report any that they become aware of.

John W.E. Harris, George Broome
Vancouver Island
Trails Information Society (VITIS)
www.hikingtrailsbooks.com

About the Editor

Outdoor writer, hiker, photographer and angler, Richard K. Blier has explored Vancouver Island trails, backroads, campsites, lakes and coastlines for over 25 years. He is the author of three guidebooks: *ISLAND ADVENTURES: An Outdoors Guide to Vancouver Island* (Orca Book Publishers, 1989, now out of print); *MORE ISLAND ADVENTURES Volume 2: An Outdoors Guide to Vancouver Island* (Orca Book Publishers, 1993); and *ISLAND BACKROADS: Hiking, Camping and Paddling on Vancouver Island* (Orca Book Publishers, 1998). He has also revised and edited

Photo courtesy of Sally McCausland

HIKING TRAILS II: South-Central Vancouver Island and the Gulf Islands (7th & 8th editions), published by the Vancouver Island Trails Information Society. (*HIKING TRAILS II* took second place in the book category of the Outdoor Writers of Canada's Communications Awards in 2001.) Mr. Blier is a backroads feature writer for *BC Outdoors Sport Fishing* magazine. Over the years his outdoor stories and photos have appeared in magazines and newspapers, including *The Islander (Victoria Times/Colonist).* You are invited to visit his **BACKROAD ADVENTURES ON VANCOUVER ISLAND** website at
http://members/shaw.ca/richardblier.